Writing Machines
N. Katherine Hayles

DESIGNER
Anne Burdick

EDITORIAL DIRECTOR
Peter Lunenfeld

MEDIAWORK
The MIT Press
Cambridge and London
MITPRESS.MIT.EDU/MEDIAWORK

Preface

On this sultry August evening I am crammed into a seat in the Los Angeles Shrine Theater along with 3,500 other attendees to SIGGRAPH 2001, the huge computer graphics trade show. We all paid $40 to see the "Electronic Theater," an evening of computer animation where high-tech practitioners of this digital art strut their stuff. Over twenty-five selections, none more than a few minutes long, are on the bill, including clips from studio films as well as short videos from independents. When the entries come from films, they often are altered to give this insider audience a glimpse of how the effects were achieved. No audio—just visuals revealing the underlying programs that created the effects. In the Academy Award-winning animated feature film, *Shrek,* for example, as the heroes flee the fire-breathing dragon across a rope bridge and the fire snakes after them, the flames appear realistically fractal in their complexity. After seeing the scene as it appeared in the movie, we are treated to a glimpse of how the modeling was done. The fire is replaced by wire-framed spheres of decreasing size, which are then texture-mapped and fractalized to yield the final effect.

Sometimes the clips contain inside jokes and witty allusions a tech-savvy audience would appreciate. It was one of these sly moments that caught my attention and made me think of this book. The scene in *Shrek* begins when the Princess is being confronted by Robin Hood and his Merry Men and she leaps into the air to do a karate move. In this altered clip prepared especially for the SIGGRAPH audience, her figure is stopped in midair and rotated 360 degrees, an allusion to a similar moment in *The Matrix* when the same move is done by Neo, the Keanu Reeves character. Unlike Neo, however, the Princess is not the film REPRESENTATION of an actor but a computer-animated figure with no counterpart in the real world. This conflation of real-world actor with computer program is continued as the "camera" backs away, revealing a movie set as it might have appeared in the shooting of *The Matrix,* with cameras positioned around a circular stage so the footage can be spliced together to give a 360-degree view. The stage set reminds us that rotating Neo's image requires many cameras when shooting film, but can be done effortlessly with a computer program simply by rotating the perspective. Then the apparently realistic cameras are wire-framed as if they were three-dimensional objects within a computer SIMULATION, which indeed they are. In this dizzying procession of images, a simulation (the Princess) has been converted to a representation (the Princess being filmed by cameras) and re-converted back to a simulation (wire-framing the cameras)—all within a matter of a few seconds, flashing by so quickly the audience scarcely has time to laugh.

The sequence illustrates that which Richard Grusin and Jay Bolter have called REMEDIATION, the cycling of different MEDIA through one another. These processes are going on all around us, including computer screens being arranged to look like television screens, television screens with multiple windows made to look like computer screens, print books mimicking computers, computers being imaged to look like books. One term put forward to describe these complex relationships is MEDIAL ECOLOGY. The phrase suggests that the relationships between different media are as diverse and complex as those between different organisms coexisting within the same ecotome, including mimicry, deception, cooperation, competition, parasitism, and hyperparasitism.

These robust interactions between media suggest a different take on the relationship between representation and simulation than that famously proposed by Jean Baudrillard more than two decades ago. Broadly speaking, representation assumes a referent in the real world, however mediated; there is an actor playing the role of Neo, although the actor of course is not the same as the character. In simulation, the referent has no counterpart in the real world; there is no actor playing the Princess, only ones and zeros in a machine. Baudrillard writes about the "precession of simulacra" as a teleological progression, resulting in an inevitable "implosion" of the real into the hyperreal, a realm in which there can be no distinction between reality and simulation because everything is already a simulation. But the cycling back and forth between representation and simulation in the SIG-GRAPH *Shrek* clip suggests that we are not so much racing toward a final implosion as participating in an ecology in which one medium is remediated in another, only to be remediated in turn.

If simulation is becoming increasingly pervasive and important, however, MATERIALITY is as vibrant as ever, for the computational engines and artificial intelligences that produce simulations require sophisticated bases in the real world. The engineers who design these machines, the factory workers who build them, the software designers who write programs for them, and the technicians who install and maintain them have no illusions that physical reality has faded away. If representation is an increasingly problematic concept, materiality offers a robust conceptual framework in which to talk about *both* representation and simulation as well as the constraints and enablings they entail.

This book is an experiment in forging a vocabulary and set of critical practices responsive to the full spectrum of signifying components in print and electronic texts by grounding them in the materiality of the literary artifact. While commenting upon a variety of cultural phenomena, it offers extensive engagement with three different kinds of literature: an electronic work by Talan Memmott entitled *Lexia to Perplexia;* an artist's book by Tom Phillips called *A Humument;* and Mark Danielewski's print novel *House of Leaves*. These texts range from coterie literature with *Lexia to Perplexia,* to a more widely read but still specialized book in *A Humument,* to a best-selling novel like *House of Leaves*. Together they demonstrate that materialist strategies are important across the board, from works aimed at esoteric readerships to those engaging mass audiences. The different media in which these works are instantiated provide the occasion for Media-Specific Analysis, a mode of critical interrogation alert to the ways in which the medium constructs the work and the work constructs the medium. As part of the Mediawork series, this book attempts to practice what it preaches by being attentive to its own material properties. As the author of the verbal text, I speak the words, but these are only part of the message; my collaborator Anne Burdick speaks in another mode through her design. The theoretical framework is mine, but my collaboration with Anne has deeply affected how I think about the interaction of verbal and visual components and so has influenced the verbal text as well.

The book is also an encoded record of a decade-long journey I have made as I moved from an orientation based in traditional literary criticism to one that took seriously my long-standing interests in technology from a literary point of view. It has long been clear to me that materiality entered importantly into the theoretical debates and technical practices of CYBERNETICS, as I argued in How We Became Posthuman: Virtual Bodies in Cybernetics, Literature and Informatics. How materiality affected literature was something I was learning as I followed the theoretical debates surrounding ELECTRONIC LITERATURE and its development from FIRST-GENERATION HYPERTEXTS into fully multimedia works. I saw in electronic literature the opportunity to think more rigorously about interactions between content and digital environments; I also believed these insights could be reflected back onto print to see it more clearly as well. This book is frankly experimental both in its format and ideas. In the zesty, contentious, and rapidly transforming medial ecology of the new millennium, it would be hubris for anyone to believe she had the definite take on anything. If Anne and I open a path or two that others may find profitable to pursue, we will in our own terms have succeeded. As is so often the case with HYPERTEXT, the rest is up to you.

CHAPTER 1   Media and Materiality

I worked in academia a decade before I realized that the bureaucratic, medieval, and wonderful institutions called universities have two ways of operating. One is dictated by administrative structures and codified rules. The other way, penetrating the first at every point, runs through networks of people and is determined by the folks who are hiring and firing, interpreting policies and setting them, approving curricula changes or not. If you really want to understand why a department gave Professor X tenure and kicked out Professor Y, you will not find the answer—or rather, the complete answer—in the handbook specifying tenure criteria. Only when you know the people in the department will you begin to see the fuller picture. The same holds true for the creative works, theories, and practices that constitute the world of literary studies. On the one hand is the skein of words, images, and artifacts that operate according to a complex dynamic of tradition and innovation, competition, and cooperation. On the other are the writers, critics, and theorists who produce the artifacts. While no one person working alone can swing that small universe one way or another, individuals matter in determining its trajectory, and networks of people matter even more.

In this experiment called *Writing Machines*, exploring what the print book can be in the digital age, only part of the story lies in the theories, concepts and examples articulated here. Another part, obvious from the moment you lay eyes on the book, inheres in its visual design. Still another is comprised by the people initiating change and resisting it, writing books and creating digital environments, struggling to see what electronic literature means and ignoring its existence altogether. Telling a fuller story requires these narrative chapters interrogating the author's position, her background and experiences, and especially the community of writers, theorists, critics, teachers, and students in which she moves. Having become an autobiographer almost against my will, I am reminded of Henry Adams' satiric admiration of Rousseau's determination in the *Confessions* that he will reveal everything about his life, from his masturbatory practices to his most wretched night thoughts. An intensely private person whose life was forever marked by his wife's suicide, Adams could not conceive indulging in such self-display. He held up his third-person character Henry Adams as a stick figure to be dressed in the fashion of the times, a shield to protect him when he was in the grave, concealing as much as it revealed and marked by multilayered ironies. If Rousseau ranks as a ten in self-display and Adams a one, I come in somewhere around three, certainly much closer to Adams' horror than Rousseau's narcissism. Insofar as my life experiences can be of interest to anyone outside my immediate family and friends, it is because they are characteristic of the transition generation raised and formed by print but increasingly molded by electronic environments. The focal points, media and materiality, will be the same as for the rest of the book but in a different voice. I am under no illusions that I can write myself, for so many reasons I cannot list them all here, from the inevitability of partial perspective to the passing of time that makes the person who writes incrementally or vastly different from the one written. Although there are autobiographical elements in the persona who will be written in these narrative chapters, no one should confuse her with me. To mark that crucial difference, she needs a name related to mine but not the same. I will call her—Kaye.

To understand Kaye's position, we need to know something about her background. She was raised in a small town in northeastern Missouri, an easy hour's drive along limestone bluffs to the Hannibal of Mark Twain fame and three hours north of St. Louis. The town was called Clarence, named along with Annabel and Leonard for the children of the brakeman who rode the Union Pacific Railroad that cut this hometown of a thousand souls in half like a butcher knife cleaving an apple. Every once in a while someone would get killed on those tracks—the town drunk who had a hobby of racing the train and one night lost to his puffing opponent, or the disgruntled husband who parked his pickup on the tracks after discovering his wife had run off with his best friend. In a place where everyone not only recognized Kaye but the model and make of the family car, there was little likelihood she could come to harm, so she was allowed to roam freely throughout the town and surrounding countryside. The experience gave her a lifelong love of the outdoors and a vivid sense of the world's materiality. She delighted in the richness of her physical environment, wealthy in tadpoles swimming in the water collected in the foundation of a ruined house, the crawdads she could tease out of the ditch by pushing a stick down their holes, the buckeyes she collected and shelled so she could watch them turn brown on her window sill. Not all her pleasures were innocent. She blushed to remember the evil day she and her older brother armed each fist with a crawdad and, claws snapping, chased their mother screaming through the house.

Offsetting these pleasures, guilty and not, was the paucity of intellectual stimulation. Although dinner conversations at home were invariably lively and wide-ranging, the small town offered little other food for the mind. School was unbelievably boring, and the local gossip was much too preoccupied with the latest scandal of the minister sleeping with the widow to talk about the political events of the day, much less larger intellectual issues. So she early turned to books, finding in them the range of experience, intensity of thought, and expanse of imagination missing in her tiny midwestern town. Her life was lived on two planes, both vivid in different ways—the everyday world of family, friends, and school, and the larger and in many ways more exciting realm of imaginative literature. By adolescence she exhausted all the reading material in the house and everything of interest in the town library, an antiquated brick building with a lofty tin ceiling and the town jail—all two cells of it—in the back. Occasionally a new book would float within her grasp. Her seventh-grade history teacher, recognizing her intellectual precociousness, gave her Lao Tzu's *The Way*, a book so remote from her experience that for the first time since she learned to read she could not make the words cohere into meaning.

Newspapers meant the *Clarence Courier*, a weekly dominated by such breaking news as Mrs. Floyd Jones having afternoon tea with Mrs. Robert Smith, where a jellyroll was served and enjoyed by all. She did not see a dial telephone until she left home for college; in Clarence she used the phone by cranking the ringer, whereupon Delores, the town operator, would answer and ask what number she wanted, no doubt continuing to listen in to catch the juicy bits. Television, like all things technological, came late to the little town, arriving a good decade after it had hit the big cities of St. Louis and Kansas City. The family purchased its first set when she was nine, and she still remembers staring at test patterns, sitting through Howdy Doody, and watching Cowboy Jim gulp down Prairie Farm milk. Aside from such occasional treats as *Science Fiction Theater* and Elvis on the Ed Sullivan show, the fare was much too thin to hold her attention for long, as were the B-Westerns shown at the Royal Theater on Saturday nights. Certainly they

Subliminal additions
in TYPE –
? of collABorator

could not compare with the books she continued to devour, accessible to her because they were low-tech and portable enough to withstand the dunking they received on occasion when she grabbed the soap. Yes, she read in the bathtub. She read everywhere, in every conceivable position. Books, paper, and ink made up her environment as much as the Midwestern land-scape that seeped deep into her bones and would always look like home. With Derrida, she could say, "Le papier, c'est moi."

As she matured intellectually, the vibrancy of the physical world returned in more sophisticated form in her science and mathematics classes, the only part of the high school curriculum that demanded real thought from her. To be sure, incompetence and mediocrity could strike even here. She sat stupefied before a physics teacher who evacuated the school's antique bell jar with a paper clip suspended at the top so he could demonstrate there is no gravity in a vacuum. After class she self-righteously marched to the principal's office to demand the teacher's resignation—she was given to such gestures in those days—but it had already been decided the teacher would not do, and the poor fellow slunk out of town on the midnight train. The mishap could not spoil science's grand attraction. She was fascinated by the underlying regularities so cleanly exposed by the laws of motion, the periodic table she memorized at sixteen, the geometric theorems that became more entrancing as they grew more difficult, and the complexities of calculus to which she and her best friend were introduced in a special tutorial her senior year.

It was inevitable that when she entered college, the only two options she really considered were science and literature. Chance drew her to Rochester, New York, where she enrolled in the Rochester Institute of Technology, a rapidly developing school that had recently received accreditation. Faced with a limited curriculum and no humanities majors, she decided upon chemistry. Immersed for the first time in an intellectual environment that could absorb all the mental horsepower she could rev up, she was in a constant state of exhilaration, so delighted to be racing along at full throttle that she only occasionally missed the literature that had sustained her for so many years. She had little free time in the

demanding curriculum that required long hours in the laboratory. Still, she could not help buying a novel every now and then, devouring it in guilty pleasure through a long night that stretched toward dawn if the book was big, squinting through the last hundred blurry pages in the wavering light of her bedside lamp.

Mediation came to her most vividly, then, not through the television her apartment did not have, or the newspapers she had no time to read, or the movies she could not afford on her frugal budget, but in the chemistry laboratory. If only she could peer at the molecules and see exactly what they were, how they moved and coupled with one another, how they arranged themselves in space and time as the reactions proceeded! The desire to see them was so intense she dreamed about it, sure that misconceptions and hazy notions would be dispelled if she could only encounter them directly. She reminded herself sternly this was science, not fiction, and the only way she could get at them was through the layers of mediation created by the laboratory equipment and procedures. She learned to speak and write precisely, careful to state no more than she could actually demonstrate, learning from mistakes and bad guesses to be wary of her conclusions to the point of eschewing all generalization (or almost all, the qualifier the lingering mark of that early education).

The move to graduate school at Caltech put her in a different class of students and teachers. Now it was not a question of revving up but keeping up as she worked alongside the brightest and best the nation—indeed, the international community—had to offer. As she began completing her course work, she found herself becoming restive. The clarity she prized and the deep explanations were as thrilling as ever, but the focus became increasingly narrow as she spent less time in classes and more time in the research laboratory coming to realize what every practicing scientist knows, that laboratory science is 95 percent mundane exacting work and 5 percent inspiration. In an odd way this environment began to seem less like a release from parochialism than a return to it, living within narrowly defined boundaries where large questions are ruled out of bounds. Perhaps the problem lay in her particular research, she thought, so she began questioning her peers at lunchtime to find out more about their research. What is it about, she would ask, and her colleagues gave eloquent and detailed answers. But when she asked them the questions that were bothering her—why is it important? what does it mean?—they laughed or shrugged them off, looking at her as if she had committed a breach of decorum. She knew, of course, that cutting-edge research was going on all around her and that it sometimes led to momentous conclusions, but she began to suspect this was the exception rather than the rule—the reward for long years of laboring day after day on work that seemed stubbornly to resist the penetration of human thought into resistant materiality. As Evelyn Fox Keller has wittily observed, it is hard work to make nature obey the laws of nature. Kaye did not mind hard work, in fact thrived on it, but she yearned to ask the big questions.

So she began to flirt with the idea of returning to her other love, literature. She took some of the few literature courses offered and had the good fortune (bad fortune for her scientific career) to encounter two gifted teachers, each great in a different way and oddly with the same surname. From Hallett Smith she was given the magnificent gift of a private tutorial in English Renaissance literature, not through any merit of her still-naive literary intelligence but from the simple fact that the workload was so strenuous the other students dropped out. Hallett Smith knew things her scientific teachers did not, but his mind worked along the same lines, valuing clarity, accuracy of information, careful reasoning, and depth of analysis. Through David Smith she encountered the literature known as the American Renaissance, and with it a mind that worked in entirely different ways from those to which she was accustomed. Ambiguity was valued over clarity, and while fascinating mysteries were posed, the point seemed to be to experience rather than explain them. It was her first encounter with a certain kind of literary sensibility, and it left a lifetime mark on her thinking. She never abandoned her commitment to precise explanation, feeling that if she really understood something she should be able to explain it to others so it was clear to them. But she began to realize that the literary game might be played in very different ways from the scientific enterprise.

The realization hit her up the side of the head with the force of a two-by-four after she entered graduate school in English, a story too removed from media and materiality to be of interest here. One memory encapsulating this third and most painful part of her education surfaces to sum up its implications. After she had completed her Ph.D. and taken her first academic job at an Ivy League college, she was standing on the steps of the English building—a House as it is called in those circles, though it was far from harboring the close-knit intimacy of the family home she had known. The afternoon sun slanted on her face, and she felt a moment of pure physical pleasure, so welcome after a long, stressful East Coast winter of coping with new colleagues, a new environment, and the parochialism that continued to follow her like an old ailment she couldn't shake. It was a kind of parochialism new to her, consisting of making finer and finer discriminations until most of the world was excluded, including public universities, technical institutions, regional colleges and all the zesty, unpredictable things happening in them, but she had no trouble in recognizing it as parochialism nevertheless. One of her colleagues, a man who spoke in long monologues she found almost impossible to follow, approached her and said in an accusing tone, "You know, the trouble with you is that you think you are solving problems." She was startled by the indictment's accuracy and could only plead guilty. "That's exactly what I think I am doing," she responded. "What are you doing?" "I," he said proudly, "am investigating problematics."

It took many years for her to temper her problem-solving attitude with an appreciation for problematics, although she grew more adept at it with practice. Meanwhile it turned out she had not so much left science behind as returned to it *from another direction* as she initiated work in literature and science, a field that *scarcely as yet existed* and that continued to involve her in questions of materiality. When she first encountered the desktop computer and understood it could be used to create literary texts, she realized that everything important to her met in the nexus of this material-semiotic object. It called forth the questions that continued to fascinate her about scientific research: what does it mean? why is it important? It confronted her with the materiality of the physical world and its mediation through technological apparatus. When used for electronic literature, it gave her the same keen pleasure as the print novels she loved, though through different sensory and kinesthetic modalities. It was over-determined that she would want to get her hands into it. The challenge, she understood even at this early moment, would be to bring together the binaries that had somehow always been important to her life: media and materiality; science and literature; immersion in an imaginative realm and delight in the physical world; the strict requirements for precisely written CODE and the richness of NATURAL LANGUAGE; underlying regularities and the free-form of creative play. She was hooked.

CHAPTER 2   Material Metaphors, Technotexts, and Media-Specific Analysis

Why have we not heard more about materiality? Granted, there have been some promising beginnings and a host of materially-based studies in the emerging field of science studies. But within the humanities and especially in literary studies, there has traditionally been a sharp line between representation and the technologies producing them. Whereas art history has long been attentive to the material production of the art object, literary studies has generally been content to treat fictional and narrative worlds as if they were entirely products of the imagination. Significant exceptions include the tradition of artists' books and the exuberant experiments of such materially-based practices as concrete poetry. A few theorists attentive to these developments have argued eloquently for the importance of the book as a physical object and for criticism as material practice. Yet they remain the exception rather than the rule. By and large literary critics have been content to see literature as immaterial verbal constructions, relegating to the specialized fields of bibliography, manuscript culture, and book production the rigorous study of the materiality of literary artifacts. Even cultural studies, refreshingly alert to the importance of materiality in cultural productions, has made only an incremental difference, largely because it usually considers artifacts outside the literary text rather than the text itself as a material object.

As the vibrant new field of electronic textuality flexes its muscle, it is becoming overwhelmingly clear that we can no longer afford to ignore the material basis of literary production. Materiality of the artifact can no longer be positioned as a subspecialty within literary studies; it must be central, for without it we have little hope of forging a robust and nuanced account of how literature is changing under the impact of information technologies. Not only electronic literature but virtually all historical periods and genres are affected as print works are increasingly re-produced as electronic documents.

The loyal opposition has been insisting for some time now that literary studies must expand to include images. The respected critic, W. J. T. Mitchell, has forcefully made this point, urging that we think not only about words but what he calls the textimage, words and images together. In the digital age, however, image is the tip of the iceberg. In a stimulating exchange I had with Mitchell, I was surprised to find him defending the position that although image was of course important, the expansion of literary attention should stop there. Once image has been introduced into the picture (so to speak), literary critics have everything they need to deal adequately with literary texts. This print-centric view fails to account for all the other signifying components of electronic texts, including sound, animation, motion, video, kinesthetic involvement, and software functionality, among others. Moreover, it does not do justice even to print books, as the vibrant tradition of artists' books testifies with the innovative use of cutouts, textures, colors, movable parts, and page order, to name only a few.

MATERIAL METAPHORS

What would it mean to talk about materiality in an era in which simulations are everywhere around us?

I found a clue in Greg Egan's brilliant novel *Permutation City,* a book I love to hate because it challenges almost everything I thought I knew about materiality. The novel begins by enacting the scenario that techno-fabulist Hans Moravec proposes in *Mind Children: The Future of Robotic Intelligence*—downloading human consciousness into a computer. Unlike Moravec, Egan does not find it necessary to destroy the original in creating the SIMULACRUM. Moreover, the Copy does not find himself identical with his biological progenitor as Moravec supposes. Depressed at becoming an artificial intelligence without a body, Copy after Copy commits suicide. Those that reconcile themselves to living inside the computer often create INTERFACES that allow them to preserve the illusion of ordinary human existence. For example, a CEO creates a boardroom with video screens through which he can interface with the far-flung business empire legally transferred to the Copy upon the original's biological death. In a sense the interface is a metaphor, for the character is not actually in a boardroom but merely interacting with the world through functionalities similar to a boardroom's operation. Nevertheless, this metaphor has power to make things happen in the real world, for it is connected to a complex material apparatus that operates machinery as well as such socio-material constructions as economic transactions.

Traditionally metaphor has been defined as a verbal figure. Derived from a root meaning bearing across, it denotes the transfer of sense associated with one word to another. In Egan's fictional scenario, the transfer takes place not between one word and another but rather between a symbol (more properly, a network of symbols) and material apparatus. This kind of traffic, as old as the human species, is becoming increasingly important as the symbol-processing machines we call computers are hooked into networks in which they are seamlessly integrated with apparatus that can actually do things in the world, from the sensors and actuators of mobile robots to the semiotic-material machinery that changes the numbers in bank accounts. To account for this traffic I propose *material metaphor*, a term that foregrounds the traffic between words and physical artifacts.

We are not generally accustomed to think of a book as a material metaphor, but in fact it is an artifact whose physical properties and historical usages structure our interactions with it in ways obvious and subtle. In addition to defining the page as a unit of reading, and binding pages sequentially to indicate an order of reading, are less obvious conventions such the opacity of paper, a physical property that defines the page as having two sides whose relationship is linear and sequen-

tial rather than interpenetrating and simultaneous. To change the physical form of the artifact is not merely to change the act of reading (although that too has consequences the importance of which we are only beginning to recognize) but profoundly to transform the metaphoric network structuring the relation of word to world.

This was the informing realization of "The Future of Reading" at San Jose's Tech Museum of Innovation (2001) mounted by the Research in Experimental Documents (RED) team at Xerox PARC, which included such pioneering thinkers as Richard Gold and Anne Balsamo. To understand the power of material metaphors, let us consider one of the reading machines the RED group built for the exhibit, the Reading Eye Dog. Designed to look like a large robotic upright dog, this mechanism scans printed material placed on its reading stand and uses a text-to-speech program to speak the words aloud. The metaphoric associations put into play by the device's physical form include traffic between machine and biological organism, companion animal and parent, printed marks and oral production, static book and dynamic text-to-speech generation, artificial intelligence and human cognition, reading text without understanding it and (for young children listening to the Reading Eye Dog), understanding what is said without being able to read it. All these associations are structured by the materiality of the artifact and differ significantly from the structuring associations called forth by the print book. To change the material artifact is to transform the context and circumstances for interacting with the words, which inevitably changes the meanings of the words as well. This transformation of meaning is especially potent when the words reflexively interact with the inscription technologies that produce them.

Here I should specify what I mean by **INSCRIPTION TECHNOLOGIES**. In print books words are obviously inscriptions because they take the form of ink marks impressed on paper. The computer also counts as an inscription technology, because it changes electric polarities and correlates these changes with binary code, higher-level languages such as C++ and Java, and the phosphor gleams of the cathode ray tube. *To count as an inscription technology, a device must initiate material changes that can be read as marks*. Telegraphy thus counts; it sends structured electronic pulses through a wire (material changes that can be read as marks) and connects these pulses with acoustic sound (or some other analogue signal) associated with marks on paper. Additional examples include film, video, and the images produced by medical devices such as X-rays, CAT scans, and MRI. Even nanotechnology slouched its way toward inscription when scientists arranged molecules to form their company's logo, IBM.

TECHNOTEXTS

When a literary work interrogates the inscription technology that produces it, it mobilizes reflexive loops between its imaginative world and the material apparatus embodying that creation as a physical presence.

Not all literary works make this move, of course, but even for those that do not, my claim is that *the physical form of the literary artifact always affects what the words (and other semiotic components) mean*. Literary works that strengthen, foreground, and thematize the connections between themselves as material artifacts and the imaginative realm of verbal/semiotic signifiers they instantiate open a window on the larger connections that unite literature as a verbal art to its material forms. To name such works, I propose "technotexts," a term that connects the technology that produces texts to the texts' verbal constructions. Technotexts play a special role in transforming literary criticism into a material practice, for they make vividly clear that the issue at stake is nothing less than a full-bodied understanding of literature.

My title, *Writing Machines*, plays with the multiple ways in which writing and materiality come together. "Writing machines" names the inscription technologies that produce literary texts, including printing presses, computers, and other devices. "Writing machines" is also what technotexts do when they bring into view the machinery that gives their verbal constructions physical reality. As a literary term, technotext can be understood through its similarities and differences to related concepts. All of the technotexts I discuss in this book could also be called hypertexts. Hypertext has at a minimum the three characteristics of MULTIPLE READING PATHS, CHUNKED TEXT, and some kind of LINKING MECHANISM to connect the chunks. The World Wide Web, with its links, millions of pages and multiple reading paths, is a vast hypertext of global proportions. From the definition, it will be immediately apparent that hypertext can be instantiated in print as well as electronic media. A print encyclopedia qualifies as a hypertext because it has multiple reading paths, a system of cross-references that serve as linking mechanisms, and chunked text in entries separated typographically from one another. These hypertextual characteristics of the encyclopedia form the basis for Milorad Pavić's brilliant print work *Dictionary of the Khazars: A Lexicon Novel*. Other examples of print hypertexts include Ursula LeGuin's *Always Coming Home*, which includes audio tapes to document a richly imagined science fiction world; Paul Zimmerman's artist's book *High Tension*, which creates a multiplicity of reading paths through an unusual physical form that allows the reader to fold diagonally cut leaves to obtain different combinations of text and image; and Robert Coover's "The Babysitter," a short story that pushes toward hypertext by juxtaposing contradictory and nonsequential events suggesting many simultaneously existing time lines and narrative unfoldings.

oulipo

As hypertext theory developed during the late 1980s and early to mid-1990s, theorists such as George Landow, Jay Bolter, Michael Joyce, and others emphasized the importance of the link, which tended to loom larger than hypertext's other characteristics. This orientation was consistent with first-generation electronic hypertexts such as Joyce's *Afternoon, a story*, an almost exclusively verbal work that employs Storyspace software to link one screen of text (or LEXIA) with another through "hot words" the reader can activate by clicking. Although this structure departs from print in providing multiple reading paths, it preserves the basic print convention of moving through a text by going from one page/screen to another. In retrospect the revolutionary claims made for these early hypertexts appear inflated, for they were only beginning to tap into the extraordinary resources offered by electronic environments.

As the technology changed, and especially as the Web grew in size, scope, and functionality, writers began to move away from the Storyspace interface to explore the rich diversity of interfaces available in such commercial software packages as Flash, Shockwave, and Dreamweaver and also HTML, VRML, DIRECTX, and other web-oriented languages. A new breed of SECOND-GENERATION ELECTRONIC LITERATURE began to appear that looked very different from its predecessors, experimenting with ways to incorporate narrative with sound, motion, animation, and other software functionalities. Riding on the crest of these developments, Espen Aarseth's pioneering *Cybertext: Perspectives on Ergodic Literature* argued for a perspective fundamentally computational in nature. To this end he proposed the category CYBERTEXT and defined it to include a wide variety of texts that used combinatorial strategies, including print works such as Raymond Queneau's *Cent Mille Milliards*, electronic fictions like *Afternoon, a story*, computer games, and even the *I Ching*. He gave substance to the idea by developing a typology of semiotic variables, including in addition to links such concepts as perspective, access, determinability, transience, dynamics, and user function. Combinations of these variables yield 576 different variations, which can be plotted on a grid to locate a particular text's strategies within the cybertext domain. This schema is undoubtedly more appropriate to second-generation electronic literature than earlier hypertext theory, which now began to appear dated and provincial compared to Aarseth's flexible and theoretically powerful approach. Meanwhile, other critics and writers who continue to be interested in linking have developed theoretically sophisticated ways to talk about hypertext that move considerably beyond the first generation of hypertext theorists.

These developments have invested hypertext and cybertext with connotations that make them useful relatives to technotext but also significantly different from what I have in mind when I use that term. Hypertext connotes an emphasis on links, a brand of criticism derived from traditional literary approaches, and a polemic that seeks to convince the literary community of the value and importance of electronic hypertext for pedagogy, criticism, and theory. Cybertext connotes a functional and semiotic approach that emphasizes a computational perspective, a polemic that wants, as Stuart Moulthrop put it (echoing James Joyce), to "kill the literary priest," and an emphasis on computer games as paradigmatic examples of ERGODIC texts, which Aarseth defines as those literary systems that require "nontrivial effort" to allow the user to traverse them. To use one term or the other is not only to invoke a particular approach but to position oneself in a highly contested field where allies and enemies sometimes count more than arguments. Neither term pays particular attention to interactions between the materiality of inscription technologies and the inscriptions they produce. As a consequence, neither term is completely appropriate to my project, although I will use both on occasions when their connotations are appropriate to the point at hand.

i.e. genre

MEDIA-SPECIFIC ANALYSIS

Complementing the foundational concepts of material metaphors, inscription technologies and technotexts is a kind of criticism that pays attention to the material apparatus producing the literary work as *physical* artifact.

Although material criticism is highly developed in specialized fields such as bibliographic criticism and textual studies, I think its value is much more general and widespread. Accordingly, I want to call it media-specific analysis (MSA), as a way to invite theorists and critics to think more broadly about the connections between strands of criticism that have not yet made common cause with one another.

Lulled into somnolence by five hundred years of print, literary studies have been slow to wake up to the importance of MSA. Literary criticism and theory are shot through with unrecognized assumptions specific to print. Only now, as the new medium of electronic textuality vibrantly asserts its presence, are these assumptions clearly coming into view. In his influential essay "From Work to Text," Roland Barthes uncannily anticipated electronic hypertext by associating text with dispersion, multiple authorship, and RHIZOMATIC structure. In positioning text against work, Barthes was among those who initiated semiotic and performative approaches to discourse, arguably one of the most important developments in literary studies in the last century. But this shift has entailed loss as well as gain. Useful as the vocabulary of text was in expanding textuality beyond the printed page, it also had the effect, in treating everything from fashion to fascism as a semiotic system, of eliding differences in materiality. Perhaps now, after the linguistic turn has yielded so many important insights, it is time to turn again to a careful consideration of what difference the materiality of the medium makes.

In calling for MSA, I do not mean to advocate that media should be considered in isolation from one another. On the contrary, media constantly engage in a RECURSIVE dynamic of imitating each other, incorporating aspects of competing media into themselves while simultaneously flaunting the advantages their own forms of mediation offer. Voyager's now-defunct line of "Expanded Books," for example, offered readers the opportunity to dog-ear electronic pages. Another option inserted a paper clip on the screenic page, itself programmed to look as much as possible like print. On the other side of the screen, many print texts are now imitating electronic hypertexts. These range from John Barth's *Coming Soon!* and Don DeLillo's *Underworld* to Bolter and Grusin's *Remediation*, which self-consciously pushes toward hypertext through arrows that serve as visual indications of hypertextual links. MSA attends both to the specificity of the form—the fact that the Voyager paper clip is an image rather than a piece of bent metal—and to citations and imitations of one medium in another. MSA moves from the language of text to a more precise vocabulary of screen and page, digital program and analogue interface, code and ink, mutable image and durable mark, computer and book.

One area where MSA can pay especially rich dividends is in hypertext theory. Some theorists working in the area of electronic literature argue that hypertext ought to be reserved for digital works. In my view, this is a mistake (and not one that cybertext theory makes). When Vannevar Bush, widely credited with the invention of the form, imagined a hypertextual system more than fifty years ago, it was not electronic but mechanical. His 1945 article, "As We May Think," testifies that it is possible to implement hypertext in a variety of ways, not only through the "go to" commands that comprise the hypertext link in digital computers. If we restrict the term hypertext to digital media, we lose the opportunity to understand how a rhetorical form mutates when it is instantiated in different media. The power of MSA comes from holding one term constant across media (in this case, technotexts) and varying the media to explore how medium-specific possibilities and constraints shape texts. Understanding literature as the interplay between form, content, and medium, MSA insists that texts must always be embodied to exist in the world. The materiality of those EMBODIMENTS interacts dynamically with linguistic, rhetorical, and literary practices to create the effects we call literature.

In attending to the materiality of the medium, MSA explicitly refutes the concept of the literary work that emerged from eighteenth-century debates over copyright and that has held considerable sway since then, although not without contestations. As Mark Rose has shown in his important book *Authors and Owners: The Invention of Copyright*, legal theorists such as Blackstone defined a literary work as consisting solely of its "style and sentiment." "These alone constitute its identity," Blackstone wrote. "The paper and print are merely accidents, which serve as vehicles to convey that style and sentiment to a distance." Subsequent commentators realized it was not practical to copyright "sentiment," for some ideas are so general they cannot be attributed to any single author: that men are mortal, for example. Rather, it was the ways in which ideas were expressed that could be secured as literary property and hence copyrighted. This judicial history, played out in a contentious environment where conflicting economic, political, and class interests fought for priority, had important consequences for literature that went beyond purely legal considerations, for it helped to solidify the literary author as a man of original genius (the author's assumed gender in these discourses was invariably male) who created literary property by mixing his intellectual labor with the materials afforded him by nature—much as Locke had argued men created private property by mixing their labor with the land. Consistently in these discourses, material and economic considerations, although they had force in the real world, were elided or erased in favor of an emphasis on literary property as an intellectual construction that owed nothing to the medium in which it was embodied. Although this conclusion was repeatedly challenged in court and in such literary movements as futurism and imagism ("No ideas but in things," William Carlos Williams declared), the long reign of print made it easy for literary criticism to ignore the specificities of the CODEX book when discussing literary texts. With significant exceptions, print literature was widely regarded as not having a body, only a speaking mind.

MSA aims to electrify the neocortex of literary criticism into recognizing that strands traditionally emphasizing materiality (such as criticism on the illuminated manuscript, on writers such as William Blake and Emily Dickinson, where embodiment is everything, and on the rich tradition of artists' books) are not exceptions but instances of MSA. Like all literature, technotext has a body (or rather many bodies), and the rich connections between its material properties and its content create it as a literary work in the full sense of the term.

Here I want to clarify what I mean by materiality. The physical attributes constituting any artifact are potentially infinite; in a digital computer, for example, they include the polymers used to fabricate the case, the rare earth elements used to make the phosphors in the CRT screen, the palladium used for the power cord prongs, and so forth. From this infinite array a technotext will select a few to foreground and

can header Be used interchageably

work into its thematic concerns. Materiality thus emerges from interactions between physical properties and a work's artistic strategies. For this reason, materiality cannot be specified in advance, as if it preexisted the specificity of the work. An emergent property, materiality depends on how the work mobilizes its resources as a physical artifact as well as on the user's interactions with the work and the interpretive strategies she develops—strategies that include physical manipulations as well as conceptual frameworks. In the broadest sense, materiality emerges from the dynamic interplay between the richness of a physically robust world and human intelligence as it crafts this physicality to create meaning.

In urging increased attention to materiality, I hope it is clear that I do not mean to argue for the superiority of electronic media. With both print and screen, the specificity of the medium comes into play as its characteristics are flaunted, suppressed, subverted, or re-imagined. Many critics see the electronic age as heralding the end of books. I think this view is mistaken. Print books are far too hardy, reliable, long-lived, and versatile to be rendered obsolete by digital media. Rather, digital media have given us an opportunity we have not had for the last several hundred years: the chance to see print with new eyes, and with it, the possibility of understanding how deeply literary theory and criticism have been imbued with assumptions specific to print. As we work toward critical practices and theories appropriate for electronic literature, we may come to renewed appreciation for the specificity of print. In the tangled web of medial ecology, change anywhere in the system stimulates change everywhere in the system. Books are not going the way of the dinosaur but the way of the human, changing as we change, mutating and evolving in ways that will continue, as a book lover said long ago, to teach and delight.

CHAPTER 3 Entering the Electronic Environment

Steeped in print literature, Kaye was like those of her generation who came to the computer as an adult. Even so, her somewhat idiosyncratic experience made her an early adopter. Her first encounter with computers predated the desktop variety by nearly two decades, for she used a computer interface to program electrodes in her scientific work. It is mind-numbingly difficult to program in ASSEMBLY CODE, and for Kaye it would always be associated with darkness. She arrived at the lab before the sun came up and left after the sun went down. Since the lab was in a sub-sub-basement, she saw precious little of that golden orb during the week. Only on weekends was she able to glory in the Southern California landscape drenched in sunlight, which soon became a second home to her.

At the Ivy League college where she served her academic apprenticeship, she encountered the equipment that before long would be called "dumb terminals," but at the time she found it thrilling to move from typewriters to this more flexible and powerful medium. At this early point terminals were not capable of full-screen response; she edited line-by-line using computer commands in a process users today would find unbearably primitive. Still idealistic enough to think she could change the world, she tried to recruit her English Department colleagues to the medium. She has a vivid memory of demonstrating the technology to a senior professor to show how easy and fun it was compared to typing and retyping drafts. He was not persuaded, begging out after fifteen minutes, saying he had other things to do (he was too polite to say, *better* things). To find colleagues who shared her enthusiasm, she went to the mathematics/computer science department, where she suggested co-teaching a master's level summer course on "Computer Literacy." At this time in the early 1980s, MODULAR PROGRAMMING was a new idea, and she thought it had much in common with the composition techniques she used in her writing classes. Paragraphs were like modules; transitions were like comments and annotations; structure and organization were like flowcharts. Why not teach advanced writing in a context that drew parallels with the modular computer programming that participants could learn at the same time? And throw into the mix some texts that would stimulate discussion about the effects of the computer revolution on print culture? Without really under-standing the implications, she already knew that the computer would drama-tically change the dynamics of what she would later learn to call medial ecology.

The connection with literature came when she received in the mail an adver-tisement from Eastgate Systems for "serious hypertext." By this time she was back in the Midwest, teaching at the University of Iowa and debating postmod-ernism with the bright eager graduate students who turned up there. She had graduated from dumb terminals to a desktop computer and couldn't wait to order Joyce's *Afternoon, a story*. She devoured it in a single setting, the way she was accustomed to do with print novels. But then it occurred to her that she had missed the point, for her reading strategy had been to use the default, which soon took her to the end—or rather, an end. Further exploration showed that the default left untouched large portions of the text. So she went back, and this time read more systematically, using the NAVIGATION tool to read all the screens, or lexias as they were called. She soon arrived at the same conclusion Jane Yellowlees Douglas was to argue later in print—that the privileged lexia, "White Afternoon," allowed the reader to see that Peter, the protagonist, was responsible for caus-ing the very accident he spends most of the narrative investigating. A clever strategy, she thought—but how would one teach a work such as this?

She tried it out with a group of college teachers from across the country when she was asked to conduct a weekend seminar for Phi Beta Kappa. Many of them made the same mistake she had, missing a lot of the text. Others argued vehemently that this electronic hypertext failed to deliver the immersion in a fic-tional world that for them was the main reason to read narrative literature. When she pointed out that many print texts, especially postmodern works, also failed to deliver this experience, they fell back on what Mark Bernstein would later call the "bathtub theory of literature," arguing that if you couldn't take the text into the bathtub with you, it wasn't worth reading. She was not entirely unsympa-thetic, for as noted earlier the tub was one of her favorite reading spots, along with being sprawled across the bed. But Kaye was not ready to concede the point. "Oh come on," she responded, "surely you cannot judge a piece of literature by such superficial standards. So what if you read it on the computer? Isn't it far more important what the language is like, the linking structure, the plot, the characters?" Later she would think back on this conversation as a classic case of the blind leading the blind, for without realizing it, she was continuing to judge this electronic text by the same criteria she used for print. It would take years and many more experiences with electronic texts before she began to understand that electronic literature operated in fundamentally different ways than print and required new critical frameworks to assess its reading and writing practices.

The mistake may have been unavoidable, not only because she had been raised on print but also because these first-generation hypertexts were largely comprised of text, making little or no use of graphics, animation, and sound. Moreover, they had relatively simple navigation systems that consisted largely of clicking on links to go from one lexia to another. Although early commentators claimed that the NONLINEAR structures and links made electronic literature qualitatively different than print books, in retrospect Kaye realized that these first-generation works were more like books than they were like second-generation electronic literature, because they operated by replacing one screen of text with another, much as a book goes from one page to another. Despite the hoopla, first-generation works left mostly untouched the unconscious assumptions that readers of books had absorbed through centuries of print. They were a brave beginning, but only a beginning. Not unlike the dumb terminals Kaye now thought of as quaint antiques, these works opened up pathways of change that would, when more fully exploited, make them seem obsolete.

Meanwhile, computer hardware and software were changing at exponential rates, and with them, ELECTRONIC LITERATURE. The text that heralded the transition to second-generation electronic literature for Kaye was Shelley Jackson's *Patchwork Girl*. It presented itself as a rewriting of Mary Shelley's *Frankenstein* in which the female monster, dismembered by a nauseated Victor in Mary's classic tale, is reassembled and made into the text's main narrator. Written in a later version of the Storyspace software that Joyce used for *Afternoon*, *Patchwork Girl* engaged the tool in significantly different ways. In an

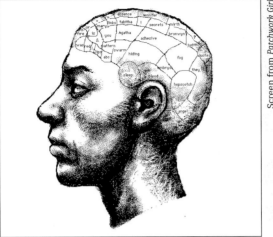

Screen from *Patchwork Girl*

important innovation, it drew connections between the electronic text and the female monster's fragmented body. One of the screens showed a large head in profile, presumably the monster's, divided into sections after the style of a phrenology chart. Clicking on them took Kaye to the stories of the women whose body parts were used to make the monster. Navigation was envisioned as taking place not only between lexias but between images and words, and more profoundly between the text and the computer producing it. This was something very different than moving from lexia to lexia; it was an effect print could not duplicate. Jackson reinforced the point by writing passages that explicitly drew connections between the machinery and the text, asking what happened to consciousness when it existed discontinuously as screens with gaps in between. Where was the narrator's consciousness during the gaps, the microseconds that separated one screen from another? Did it dissolve into the noise of the machine, decomposed back into ones and zeros?

The speculation sent chills down Kaye's spine. It was her first glimpse into how significantly literature might change if the literary body was not a book but a computer. She could name dozens of print texts that played with connections between the book and a narrator's body, from Laurence Sterne's eighteenth-century masterpiece *Tristram Shandy*, to Italo Calvino's contemporary print hypertext novel *If on a Winter's Night a Traveler*. As a print lover, she had taken for granted that the book as a physical artifact would ground metaphoric

networks connecting the print form with the bodies of characters and narrators, authors and readers. Authors regularly thought of their books as offspring; characters in metafiction often tried to peer out of the covers that contained them to see the book as an object; the human form converged with book technology even in such inert metaphors as footnotes, spine, and appendix. All this was obvious and known. But the trembler now rippling through her consciousness hinted at a shift in tectonic plates massive enough to send an earthquake roaring through the terrain of literary studies, for it implied that a shift in the material SUBSTRATE of the artifact would affect not just the mode of delivery but everything about the literary work. Like all really momentous changes, this realization came in fits and starts for Kaye, now clearly foreseen, now slipping into inarticulate intuition. She knew and yet she didn't know. It would take several shocks to her system before she grasped the fuller significances of moving from print to the computer.

The first shock was mild, even pleasant. She was invited by the University of Bergen to serve as the "First Opponent" on the dissertation defense of a young Norwegian scholar, Espen Aarseth. The procedure was a grueling full-day ordeal that bespoke the university's medieval origins. The candidate delivered a 45-minute lecture on his dissertation, which the committee judged satisfactory or not. If satisfactory, the defense proceeded to the second stage, which consisted of the First and Second Opponents questioning the candidate for a full hour each, probing for weaknesses, inconsistencies, and so on. She thought the dissertation was excellent, but she tried gamely to enter into the spirit of the exercise. When the candidate passed with flying colors, tradition called for him to host a dinner that evening, to which were invited friends, relatives, mentors, and of course the dissertation committee. Numerous toasts were made, all in Norwegian so she couldn't understand a word, but she gathered that the gist was to ridicule the academic proceedings, a sport she enjoyed even without knowing the language.

The dissertation was already accepted for publication by the Johns Hopkins University Press and would become an influential work in electronic literature. As noted earlier, Aarseth coined the term cybertext, clearing the field of previous work that had identified the link as the defining characteristic of hypertext. He argued for a computational perspective, a move that placed literary works on the same playing field as computer games and other combinatorial works. He made the important point that textual functions must not only be based on the marks appearing on screen but also had to take into account what was happening inside the machinery. To distinguish between screen display and underlying code, he coined the terms SCRIPTON and TEXTON. Here was a perspective and vocabulary that reinterpreted the print book in terms of the computer, rather than shoe-horning electronic texts into categories derived from print.

The second shock came at a Digital Arts conference in Atlanta at which she had been invited to deliver a keynote address. Usually she prepared carefully for such occasions, but the week of the conference she came down with a violent flu and spent days shaking in bed with chills and fever. A sensible person would have cancelled, but she came from good German stock where phrases like "Your word is your bond" were not only intoned but actually practiced. So she gulped down the antibiotics that her doctor had predicted would do no good and boarded the plane. Her lecture passed in a daze; she could scarcely remember what she said, and no doubt it deserved to be forgotten. The discussion that followed, however, was memorable, for it marked a turning point for Kaye. In the audience were such luminaries as Michael Joyce of *Afternoon* fame and critic Janet Murray, author of *Hamlet on the Holodeck*. They took her to task for using vocabulary and concepts that were *too literary*—the opposite of Aarseth's computational approach. She was startled to hear this objection from someone like Joyce, who was, if possible, even more steeped in the literary tradition than she and constantly used allusions to literary works in his writing, including several lexias in *Afternoon* based on James Joyce's *Ulysses*. Surely, she objected, we cannot throw out everything four centuries of literary criticism has taught us about character, plot, narration, voice? He conceded the point but remained unconvinced. He wanted something more, though he could not say exactly what.

The next shock struck closer to home. Her close friend, M. D. Coverley, had given Kaye her electronic hypertext novel *Califia*. To Kaye, M. was Margie, a wonderful person who was invariably warm and gracious, smart and perceptive. Kaye read the work and was not swept away by the narrative, finding it presentable but not overwhelming. When she conveyed this, Margie patiently pointed out features that Kaye had noticed but had not really integrated into her reading—the navigational structure, for example, which offered at least twenty different

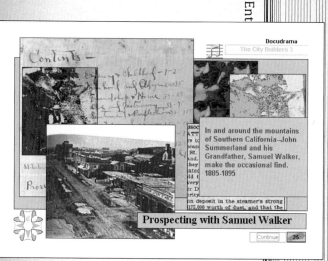

Docudrama
The City Builders 3

Contents —

In and around the mountains
of Southern California--John
Summerland and his
Grandfather, Samuel Walker,
make the occasional find.
1885-1895

on deposit in the steamer's strong
175,000 worth of dust, and that the

Prospecting with Samuel Walker

Continue   25

pathways on every screen and which, with two or three clicks, could be used to access any of the work's 800 screens. Only later, when Kaye returned to *Califia* after more than a year had passed, did she understand that her mistake had been precisely to *read* the work, concentrating mainly on the words and seeing the navigation as a way to access the words, the images as illustrations of the words. She thought more deeply about the nature of the *Califia* project, which drew connections between present-day narrators and a rich treasure trove of California history, including economics, water politics, and geology, using an astonishing variety of inscription surfaces including road maps, documents, letters, journals, and even star maps. Finally it hit her: the work embedded the verbal narrative in a topographic environment in which word was interwoven with world. The world contained the words but much else besides, including layered images, complex navigation functionalities, and simulated documents. By focusing on the words alone, she had missed the point. Now she was able to evaluate *Califia* in a different way, from an integrated perspective in which all components became SIGNIFYING PRACTICES. From this viewpoint, she could see not only that it was a ground-breaking work but also that the materiality of the text was integral to its project of connecting word with world.

This was a significantly different practice from a conventional print novel in which a world is evoked exclusively through words, and different also from an illustrated work in which words and images work together. She could not grasp

the work as a whole without taking the computer into account, with its material specificity of hardware capabilities and software functionalities. Medium and work were entwined in a complex relation that functioned as a multilayered metaphor for the relation of the world's materiality to the space of simulation. "This is deep," she thought to herself in a dawning realization that was half perplexity, half illumination. "Material metaphor," a phrase casually dropped by her anthropologist husband, swam into consciousness as an appropriate expression to describe these complexities.

The point was driven home by her encounter with Diana Slattery's *Glide*, a beautifully designed piece that speculated about what it would be like to live in a culture that had developed a VISUAL LANGUAGE that could be written and enacted but not spoken. The *Glide* site was a fully multimedia work, displaying animated GLYPHS—the components of the Glide language—transforming into one another while deep resonant chords played on the soundtrack. The narrative, extracted from Slattery's full-length print novel, *The Maze Game* (soon to be published), depicted a culture whose central ritual is the titular Game, a contest between a Dancer who runs a maze that is also a Glide message and a Player who tries to solve the maze represented as a video game. Breaking the deep connection between written mark and spoken sound, *Glide* envisioned different connections emerging between language and vision, body movement and code. Kaye saw in it a parable about the profound changes afoot as the human sensorium was reconfigured by information technologies, including electronic literature.

Now she thought she had something worthwhile to say, and when the North American Association for the Study of Romanticism invited her to give a keynote lecture, she accepted despite knowing little about English Romantic literature. The conference topic was the materiality of Romanticism, and she figured to use the occasion to convey some of her hard-won insights about the importance of materiality in literary works, the necessity for MSA, and the ways in which thinking about electronic texts could illuminate print. Brimming with good health this time, she prepared her talk with care, using visuals from the magnificent William Blake Archive on the Web to show that the electronic Blake functioned in significantly different ways than Blake in print. She further made a point of the site's rhetoric, which emphasized rendering the print Blake as exactly as possible,

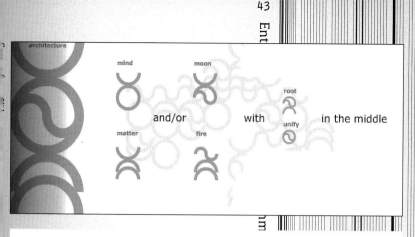

architecture

mind   moon   root

and/or   with   unify   in the middle

matter   fire

providing users with a sizing tool and color device so they could adjust their browsers. But these very functionalities were themselves part of what made the electronic Blake different than the print Blake. In her conclusion she drew the *obvious moral that the literary community could no longer afford to treat text on screen as if it were print read in a vertical position. Electronic text had its own specificities, and a deep understanding of them would bring into view by contrast the specificities of print, which could again be seen for what it was, a medium and not a transparent interface.*

By this time the argument was so obvious to her that *she was afraid it might* seem too simple. Her audience's reaction told her otherwise. As they moved into the discussion period, the room seemed to break out in a sweat. As the tension became palpable, one woman articulated it explicitly: "I want you to know how anxious you have made me," she said. Kaye was even more taken aback when W. J. T. Mitchell, the other keynote speaker whom she revered as a god, rose to express the opinion mentioned earlier: that the only two important signifying components of a literary text are words and images; nothing else really counts. Mitchell had authored the influential book *Picture Theory* arguing that literary criticism had to move away from the parochialism of considering literature to be only verbal structures; images too must be taken into account. Kaye was stunned to think he could not see that the arguments of *Picture Theory* made it important to think about a medium in all its specificity. She was sure his assertion that only words and images mattered did not hold true for electronic literature; *Califia* and *Glide* had taught her that. But she believed it did not hold true for print texts either, including virtually all artists' books.

She left the conference thinking she would have to learn more about why her audience had been so resistant to media specificity. She recalled a computer-phobic colleague who complained to Kaye about various outrages to which the computer subjected her. Kaye could sympathize to an extent; she had spent too many hours dealing with software glitches and hardware problems not to understand the woman's frustration. But she had no more power to stop the transformation of literary studies by information technology than her colleague—even if she wanted to, which she didn't. For literary people like her colleague, the computer was threatening because it demanded new skills and made traditional ones obsolete at an alarming rate. "I'm glad I am retiring soon," another colleague had remarked to her, "because now I won't have to deal with these changes."

She acknowledged the problems. It was not only the computer-phobic who suffered from their impact. She watched incredulously when Michael Joyce, a figure so esteemed in electronic literature that he was regularly referred to as "His Joyceness," announced he was leaving electronic literature and going back to print. When she wrote an urgent email asking why, he responded with an "open letter," sent to many of his colleagues and admirers, saying that he felt his continuing growth as a writer and thinker required it. Another blow was delivered by Robert Coover, a man she admired not only for his experimental print fiction but also for the stance he had taken in an influential *New York Times* article a decade ago in which he had put his considerable prestige at risk to come out in favor of hypertext literature. At the same Digital Arts conference where she had spoken, Coover stunned the audience of mostly younger writers and artists interested in pushing the envelope of the electronic medium by announcing that the Golden Age of hypertext was over and we were rapidly declining into the Silver Age, if not the Bronze and Iron.

She could not imagine why Coover would make this pronouncement, and it was several months before she had the chance to talk with him about it. He explained that for him literature was about the voice of the writer, and he feared that *voice* was being overwhelmed by the very developments that seemed so exciting to Kaye. She could see that if voice was what mattered most to you,

second-generation electronic works generally had less of it than first-generation texts and so from this perspective could be seen as a decline. It came down, she realized, to a question of what constituted literature. She was less interested in reinforcing boundaries—a consistent theme in her life—than in seeing what happened if you romped over them, which second-generation works were exuberantly doing as they moved toward multimedia, creating works that contained components drawn from literature, visual arts, computer games, and programming practices. To her, this was part of their appeal.

Coover also expressed concern about the relentless cycles of software innovation and obsolescence. He felt he could not continue to master all the new software programs coming out at an accelerating pace and still devote his energy to what he cared about most, crafting words. She could understand his reasoning and respect his position, for she knew as well as he that the marketplace was demanding and unforgiving. The personal decisions of Joyce and Coover foregrounded more general concerns that worried her about electronic literature—problems of access, obsolescence, and software compatibility, not to mention the fact it was a pricey enterprise for writers, and very few if any were making money from it.

Still, even considering these difficulties, she saw electronic literature as one of the most important literary developments since the mid-twentieth century, and she felt confident it would be a major component of the twenty-first century canon. Moreover, electronic textuality was here to stay as more print books were reconstructed for the Web, from medieval manuscripts, to illustrated works like William Blake's books, to multimedia sites devoted to such master texts as Joyce's *Ulysses*. Even if electronic literature crashed and burned, which she considered highly unlikely, literary studies could no longer pretend that electronic textuality was print on a screen. The desktop computer changed things forever. Print would never be the same as it was when she was programming assembly code in the sub-sub-basement—and neither would she.

CHAPTER 4   Electronic Literature as Technotext: *Lexia to Perplexia*

LEXIA
to

PERPLEXIA
HYPERMEDIATION | IDE

The Process of /

Double-Funnels

Metastrophe

Exe.Termination

Alan Turing gave us the hint half a century ago when he proved that the Universal Turing Machine could simulate any calculating machine, including itself. During his era the emphasis fell on the computer's calculating abilities, but he already saw that an equally important quality was its capacity for simulation. In the new millennium, the digital computer has emerged as the most powerful simulation engine ever built. Computers are much more than hardware and software. In their general form, computers are simulation machines producing *environments*, from objects that sit on desktops to networks spanning the globe. To construct an environment is, of course, to anticipate and structure the user's interaction with it and in this sense to construct the user as well as the interface. When the simulated environment takes literary and narrative form, potent possibilities arise for reflexive loops that present the user with an imaginative fictional world while simultaneously engaging her with a range of sensory inputs that structure bodily interactions to reinforce, resist, or otherwise interact with the cognitive creation of the imagined world. The MINDBODY is engaged, not merely mind or body alone. Hence the force of material metaphors, for they control, direct, and amplify this traffic between the physical actions the work calls forth and structures, and the imaginative world the artifact creates with all its verbal, visual, acoustic, kinesthetic, and functional properties.

In the electronic literary work considered in this chapter, diverse strategies are employed to create a technotext that structures users as well as environments. Because the medium is the computer, the reflexive loop circles through the computer as a simulation engine. As ARTIFICIAL LIFE researchers have argued, simulation does not necessarily mean that the processes running in a computer are artificial. The *processes* can be as "natural" as anything in the real world; they are artificial only in the sense that they run in an artificial medium. Thus the naturalness or artificiality of the environment becomes a variable to be defined by the work, not a pregiven assumption determined by the medium. In Talan Memmott's *Lexia to Perplexia*, the artificiality of the environment is foregrounded to suggest that subjects are themselves simulations operating according to the dynamics and protocols of the medium through which they are constituted. To the extent the user enters the imaginative world of this environment and is structured by her interactions with it, she also becomes a simulation, an informational pattern circulating through the global network that counts as the computational version of human community.

Memmott's work insists on the co-originary status of SUBJECTIVITY and electronic technologies. Instead of technologies being created by humans, this work imagines DIGITAL TECHNOLOGY present from the beginning, with subjects and technologies producing each other through multiple recursive loops. Divided into four sections, *Lexia to Perplexia* is less a narrative than a set of interrelated speculations about the future (and past) of human–intelligent machine interactions, along with extensive reinscriptions of human subjectivity and the human body. "The Process of Attachment" re-describes bonding and community in terms that make their formation inextricably entwined with intelligent machines. "Double-Funnels" uses iconography (eye-conography) to suggest that "local" bodies connect to "remote" bodies by comingling in and with the computer apparatus in a process appropriately called "remotional." "Metastrophe" sets forth several "minifestos" proclaiming that the future of human life lies in "communification," a coinage combining commodification with communication. "Exe.termination" provides an animated sequence of hyper words ("hyperlecture," "hyperlexia," "hypermedia," etc). along with images of written sheets. Clicking on these reveals texts that give an overview of the project's philosophy, especially the processes of "cyborganization"—transforming human subjects into hybrid entities that cannot be thought without the digital inscription apparatus that produces them.

To develop these ideas, Memmott devises an idiosyncratic language, a revisioning of classical myths, and a set of coded images that invite the reader to understand herself as a permeable membrane through which information flows. Three principal strategies enact this transformation. The first category is linguistic. Memmott devises a wide range of **NEOLOGISMS**—coinages made from existing words that express new syntheses. He also creates a **CREOLE** discourse compounded from English and computer code. (A creole, unlike **PIDGIN**, is not an amalgam but a new language that emerges when two different language communities come into contact.) The creole is formed as code erupts through the surface of the screenic text, infecting English with machine instructions and machine instructions with English, as if the distinction between natural and programming language has broken down and the two scripts are mingling promiscuously inside the computer. In addition to these linguistic strategies are rewritings of myth. Drawing on a range of classical references from the story of Echo and Narcissus to Minoan funeral practices, Memmott reenvisions this material to make it enact narratives about how human subjects misunderstand themselves as autonomous agents when in fact they cannot be separated from the information technologies that, more than expressing, co-create them. Finally, Memmott develops a symbolic visual language that images the cyborganization of human subjects, including eyes that mutate into "I-terminals," mathematical expressions that suggest human thought is being transformed into algorithms as it mingles with computer processes, and animations that remind the user she is only partially in control of the text's movements.

One way to bring these issues into focus is to notice at what points the screen displays cease to be legible as readable texts. These occluded representations create visual images that mark the limits of what human perception can discern. Illegible texts hint at origins too remote for us to access and interfaces transforming too rapidly for us to grasp. The text announces its difference from the human body through this illegibility, reminding us that the computer is also a writer, and moreover a writer whose operations we cannot wholly grasp in all their semiotic complexity. Illegibility is not simply a lack of meaning, then, but a signifier of distributed cognitive processes that construct reading as an active production of a cybernetic circuit and not merely an internal activity of the human mind.

When *Lexia to Perplexia* hovers at the border of legibility, it hints that our bodies are also undergoing metamorphoses. What we read when we cannot read is not so much the disjunction between us and the computer (for it is always possible to access the underlying code and hack our way into a readable version of the non-readable text). Rather, the occluded display signifies a trajectory in which we become part of a cybernetic circuit. Interpolated into the circuit, we metamorphose from individual interiorized subjectivities to actors exercising agency within the extended cognitive systems that include non-human actors. In this broader context, illegible text reminds us of the changes our bodies are undergoing as they are remapped and reinterpreted by intelligent machines working within networks that bind together our flesh with their electronic materiality. In this posthuman conjunction, bodies of texts and bodies of subjects evolve together in complex configurations that carry along the past even as they arc toward an open and unknown future.

Typical is the opening screen locating the origin of the self in a specular play with an Other:

> *The inconstancy of location is transparent to the I-terminal as its focus is at the screen rather than the origin of the image. It is the illusory object at the screen that is of interest to the human enactor of the process -- the ideo.satisfractile nature of the FACE, an inverted face like the inside of a mask, from the inside out to the screen is this same <HEAD> [FACE]<BODY>, <BODY> FACE </BODY> rendered now as sup|posed other.*

Read as HTML, <HEAD>[FACE]<BODY> has two opening tags but no closing tags, which would indicate that FACE is part of HEAD but is not included in BODY. A different interpretation is suggested by <BODY>FACE</BODY>, which indicates that FACE is tagged as being the BODY. These creolized puns make a serious point, for they allude to the mind/body split in which the face, the most intensely signifying part of the human form, is first associated with the head or mind and then read as part of the body.

Parsing body parts as textual components initiates a connection between flesh and electronic materiality that is further underscored by the electronic signature **Sign.mud.Fraud**. Inserting the dot references its use in program names to delimit a file extension. The dot also divides the name; it functions both as an allusion to Freud (Fraud), announcing its ironic appropriation of this seminal thinker and also punctuating (or as one of Memmott's neologism would have it, "puncturating") the signature so that it performs what cyborganization implies by transforming a proper name into creolized sign. This performance of hybridity is further reinforced by the passage's content, where the self is generated through a reflection on the *inside* of the screen, as if on "the inside of a mask." The dislocation from traditional subjectivity is here triply articulated. First the face is seen as a mask, implying an inside different from the outside, and then this traditional trope of the persona is further dislocated by metaphorically connecting the mask with the screen, so that the interiorized life of the subject is positioned *inside* the technology. Thus inside and outside, terms conventionally generating the boundaries between subject and world, are reconfigured so the subject and the techno-object are both inside, interfaced with the world through a screen that functions at once as display and reflecting surface. A third layer is added through the screen display, for as the user moves the cursor over the passage quoted above, stylized eyes appear along with terminal screens. This iconography can be read either as interiorized eyes looking out at us through the screen-mask or reflections of our own eyes looking at the screen, thus positioning the reader as Narcissus gazing at an image that he fails to recognize as himself. By implication, this narcissistic doubling positions us inside the screen as well as external to it, intimating that we too have become techno-subjects. Although this specular play obviously alludes to the Lacanian mirror stage, it differs significantly from the Imaginary self that Lacan theorized. The subject generated by the reflections between terminal and I/eye is inscribed as cell...(f) or cell.f, expressions that visually display their infection by code and hint that the subject has been fused with the technology. From this dynamic emerges the subject as an I-terminal, an expression recalling critic Scott Bukatman's punning phrase `TERMINAL IDENTITY`. Acknowledging the illusion of an autonomous I/Eye, I-terminal subverts autonomy through the hyphenated appendage that connects human vision with the scanning electrode beam of a computer display.

As we have seen, *Lexia to Perplexia* moves toward a creole devised from the merging of English with programming code. Creole expressions include the cell...f (and cell.f) noted above, homophones for self that conflate identity with a pixilated cell and the notation for a mathematical function, respectively; inTents, a pun that collapses intensity into intentionality and also references the programming practice of using interior capitalization to make clearly visible two functions in a variable name that allows no spaces; exe.stream, another pun that references and inverts the usual use of the exe. extension to denote an executable program; and *.fect, a neologism that alludes to the programming practice of using * as a wild card, so *.fect could be read as infect, defect, disinfect, etc. To what purpose is this creole concocted? Compounded of language and code, it forms the medium through which the origin of subjectivity can be re-described as coextensive with technology. Just as these hybrid articulations do not exist apart from their penetration by code, so the subject does not exist apart from the technology that produces the creole describing/creating the techno-subject.

Nowhere is this circular dynamic more on display than in Memmott's revisioning of the myth of Echo and Narcissus. About Narcissus who mistakes himself for an Other through the mediation of a reflective surface we have already heard, but Echo's role is equally important. She reacts to her exclusion from the narcissistic circuit by losing her flesh and becoming a mediated repetition of what others say. Echo is an appropriate nymph to haunt this text, for *Lexia to Perplexia* is permeated by echolaic articulations. In an email dated November 12, 2000, Memmott says that he created the text by selecting passages from such seminal thinkers as Freud, Nietzsche, Heidegger, and Deleuze and Guattari. He then "mediated" (or remediated) them by puncturating them with neologisms and creolized transformations. *primary [X] still The Basis - the mediation*

> It was my method for the development of this piece to collect a stack of books that I thought may be helpful, distracting, add to or subtract from the argument. As I passed through these volumes I would pull texts for later mediation. When there was enough text to begin this mediation work, which in fact began by the selecting of various volumes, I compiled the excerpts together and began parsing for context. So, I became I-Terminal; you, she, he became X-terminal, and so on. This made the collected texts, the analects very messy so I endeavored to rewrite only using this premediated text as reference. The context is built from the simple replacing of 'selves' and 'others' with cyborganized values. Then it is a matter of creating the connective, conductive space between.

To see the results, consider the following passage describing the appearance of Echo, associated with the collapse of the original into the simulation, so there is no longer an ONTOLOGICAL distinction between real and artificial life.

From out of NO.where, Echo appears in the private space of Narcissus.tmp to form a solipstatic community (of 1, ON) with N.tmp, at the surface. The two machines -- the originating and the simulative -- collapse and collate to form the terminal-I, a Cell.f, or, cell...(f) that processes the self as outside of itself -- in realtime.

Through the neologism, "solipstatic," the state of mental isolation denoted by solipsism is conflated with static, which in a machine context references both the inevitable intrusion of noise and the on-off functionality of the machine. In contrast to living organisms, the machine can undergo a period of inertness and still be capable of reanimation when the switch is turned on. The neologism thus combines two very different forms of intelligent life into a "solipstatic community," an oxymoron whose strong internal tensions are envisioned as springing from the combination of fleshless Echo with doubled Narcissus.

The oxymoron is then further assimilated with the programming function n.tmp, a name customarily used for a function that will be replaced by another. As the nomenclature suggests, n.tmp immediately slides into another union as the "originating" and "simulative" machines collapse into one another. If we like, we can suppose that the originating machine is the human and the simulative one the computer. But any such assignment partakes of the Imaginary, for the emergence of the I-terminal reveals that the division between the human and the technological is an origin story that narrates as a temporal process something that was always already the case. So the cell.f imagines "the self as outside of itself" in "realtime." Realtime is a phrase programmers use to indicate that the simulated time of computer processes is running, at least temporarily, along the same time scale as the real time experienced by humans. Thus the temporal language used to authenticate the evolutionary story of an originary machine separate from a simulative machine is already infected with the technological. The collapse of the simulative into the original can be imagined as an event at a discrete moment in time, but the language reveals that this narration is after the fact, for the fusion has always already happened.

The transformation of the self into a cell.f does not end with the individual subject, for the process extends from local to remote bodies. **The bi.narrative exe.change between remote and local bodies is con.gress and compressed into the space between the physical screen and the Oculus of terminal-I.** As a result, the progression into the solipstatic original is succeeded by **The cyborganization of any/every para.I-terminal** so that the individual is subsumed into the **greater X-terminal** formed **from component I-terminals.** Thus human community becomes indistinguishable from the global network of the World Wide Web. **The completion of this circuit is an applied communification -- synamatic programs and values shared by** ... **other applications and detached machines**

"Synamatic," a homophone for cinematic, perhaps alludes to the Symantec (semantic) Corporation, famed for their Norton Anti-Virus and Norton Utilities, a conflation that implies computer health is integral to the reproduction of screen image and therefore to subjectivity. Communification arises when the circuit is completed, that is when humans and intelligent machines are interconnected in a network whose reach is reinforced by naming the few exceptions "detached" machines.

The graphics accompanying these texts include, in addition to terminals and eyes, the letters E.C.H.O. dispersed across underlying text and animated rollovers that appear in quick succession, occluding portions of the screen. Particularly significant is the image of double funnels with the small ends facing each other, a sign that Memmott associates *not so diff from Brook Rose — markson*

with "intimacy," the process by which two selves (cell...fs) meet in the computer "apparatus" and, through their interactions with the apparatus, reconstitute from bits and bytes an impression of an other in a relation that Memmott appropriately neologizes as "remotional." Seen from one perspective, as Memmott points out, the cone with an elongated end is a funnel condensing the cell....f so it can circulate through the network; seen in mirror inversion, the cone becomes a megaphone, an amplifying device that lets the receiving cell...f construct an image of the sending cell...f. As Memmott makes clear in the companion work "Delimited Meshings: agency|appliance|apparatus," *Lexia to Perplexia* must be considered not only as text but as a fully multimedia work in which screen design and software functionality are part of its signifying practices. Memmott, who came to electronic textuality from a background as a painter, notes that "much of the writing is integrated with the screen design. In addition to this, much of what was written prior to the development of the hypermedia work has in fact been incorporated into the functionality of the work. Portions of the text that I thought may be better served as screen interactions do not appear at the superficial text level but inspired some of the animations as actions that occur in the piece." (email dated November 14, 2000).

These actions often surprise and frustrate a user. Slight cursor movements cause text the user was reading to disappear or become illegible as new images and symbols are superimposed on top of it. *Lexia to Perplexia* is a very "nervous" document. It constantly acts/reacts in ways that remind the user she is not in control; not only are the cursor movements extraordinarily sensitive but some of the actions are animations controlled by timed computer sequences. Eugene Thacker, commenting on a version of this essay, writes about his encounter with the work. "A first-time reader of this work is, among other things, struck by the activity of the work: like many hypertext and net.art works, it seems to be alive, sometimes frenetic, sometimes frustratingly inert, and usually hyper-sensitive to any action on the part of the READER/USER."

does this do away w "concept" why not "reader" term up self?

This dense layering of the screen display, insofar as it interferes with reading, manifests itself as a kind of noise that is simultaneously a message. The linking structure works not by moving the reader from lexia to lexia—the standard form used by first-generation literary hypertexts such as *Afternoon*—but rather through a combination of user and computer actions that nervously jump from one screen layer to another, as if probing the multiple layers of code used to produce these effects. Thus the action of *choosing* that first-generation hypertext theory attributed solely to the reader here becomes a distributed function enacted partly by the reader but also partly by the machine. Memmott interprets this design in "Delimited Meshings: agency|appliance|apparatus" as creating "a text that does what it says—confronting the user as it mimes the User's actions." The I-terminal is thus at once a theme within the work and a performance of techno-subjectivity jointly enacted by computer and user.

An important component in the process of configuring the subject as an I-terminal is noise, which can play a productive role in complex systems by forcing them to re-organize at higher levels of complexity. » MINIFESTO 1   Mar. 10 2000/ 2:15AM   seems to evoke this possibility when it proclaims, Bi.narrative communification is rendered in the wreck, the mess in the middle, the collision of incompatible transmissions, arising from the eroded ruins of miscommunication. Recalling the phrase that circulated through the post-World War II Macy Conferences on Cybernetics of the "man in the middle" (i.e., the man spliced between two automated cybernetic machines), the "mess in the middle" promises to self-organize into a new kind of message, an emergent articulation produced by subversive Secret(e) agents who produce narra(c)tive singularities throughout the apparatus.

Manifesto
deliberate ∆-

The apparatus names not only the technology but also the interpolated subjects who have become indistinguishable from electronic messages. **» MINIFESTO 2** Jan. 21 2000/ 11:00PM proclaims,

> The **Earth**'s own **active crust** we are, building, building -- up and out - antannae, towers to tele*. We *.fect the atmosphere as we move through it, construct the infosphere as we move through it, striving toward communification. Our hyperlobal expectations spread knowledge into no.ledge, far, wide, thin -- surrounded by, and so -- without. I cannot contain myself and so I spread out- pan - send out signals, smoke and otherwise, waiting ... for logos to give me a sine.

"Hyperlobal" neatly sutures lobes—presumably of the brain—into the hyperglobal expectations of a worldwide communication system, creating a technohuman hybrid. A similar conflation resonates in logos as a mathematical (sine) function and a word capable of signification (sign). If re-organization occurs, these neologisms suggest, it will operate to fuse human subjectivity with silicon processes. In fact this transformation is already underway as the creole performs what it describes, creating a narrative that reaches back to an origin already infected (or *.fected) with technology and pushes forward into a future dominated by communification.

As we learn to make sense of the creole, we are presented with an ironic description of our attempts to make everything

crystal clear and susynchronized

to reduce its POLYVOCALITY so that **the pas**
conduit is smooth, without catches or serration and the doub
combat or challenge. The combined inTents perform as comp
de.signing, de.veloping and exe.cuting the mechanism that p

At times the "doubled trans/missive agent(s)" of code and language cooperate to yield a consistent meaning, as in the neologism hyperlobal. But these moments of clarity are embedded in screen designs where they are transitory at best, flashing on the screen in quick bursts broken by animated graphics that intervene to obscure text and layer one image over another. The noise that permeates the text may serve as a stimulus to emergent complexity, but it also ensures meanings are always unstable and that totalizing interpretations impossible.

As the transformation of self into cell...f continues, the work imagines flesh becoming digitized into binary signs.

From here, the analog and slippery digits of the real are po
...

variable body, the abstracted and released cont nuum o
encoded, codified -- made elemental... Now we are sm
communification that we minimize the space of flesh

Significantly, there are no intact bodies imaged at the site, only eyes and terminals (I-terminals), along with creolized text, mathematical functions and pseudo-code. Of course, everything is already code in the programming levels of the computer, so in this sense the human body has already been "reduced and encoded, codified...made elemental." If the body of this text aspires not merely to represent the bodies of writers and readers but also to perform them, then they too become code to be compiled in a global dynamic of communification. In a startling literalization of the idea that we are bound together with the machine, this vision implies that at some point (or many points) our flesh will circulate through the cybernetic circuit, miniaturized so that it can slip through the "mouth of the funnel" and merge with other subjectivities into a collective "we."

This at least is the ideology of the text, but the actuality of its materialization is more complex. At the same time the work appears to banish the flesh, it also relies on embodiment for its digital performance. Mark Hansen drew my attention to the bodily responses necessary to actualize the homophonic puns permeating the work. For example, "inTents" references the motivations that drive the creation and consumption of the text; it also is a pun on "intense," the state of focused alertness necessary to comprehend this difficult text. Moreover, through internal capitalization it suggests that the state of in-tending can be read both as inwardness and as a trajectory "tending" toward some end, presumably communification. To decode these multiple meanings, the user needs three different sensory modalities: sight, sound, and kinesthesia. To catch the intents/intense pun, the user must "hear" the sound through subvocalization; to decode the creolized pun suggested by interior capitalization, the user must attend to the word's visual form; and to connect word with screen design, the user must move the cursor over many areas of the surface.

In a print medium, the durable inscription of ink marks on paper normally requires that only one word be written in one place. The multiple layers embedded within a single screen in *Lexia to Perplexia* routinely violate this presumption, revealing multiple encodings piled on top of one another on the same screen. The electronic medium is here

*Communication-
Communism* [handwritten]

used to create "noisy" messages, making noise itself a message about the distributed cognitive environment in which reading takes place. The nervous screen constantly challenges the user by reacting to her movements in ways she did not anticipate or intend. Against this background of bodily performance—considerably more complex than that involved in reading a traditional print work—the text proclaims "it is the hope of communification that we minimize the space of the flesh." But the text, in ironic subversion of communification, actually creates conditions of consumption that *expand* the "space of the flesh."

Similarly, the text also takes an ironic stance toward the future of "communification" when it explores its own obsolescence.

» MINIFESTO 3   Feb. 12 2000/ 1:40AM

proclaims,   The
machine is built in expectation, more than as an
object - the tangible machine, the one you are
seated before, is dead already, or returns a dead
eye -- slowly -- I can't think fast enough; or, if
today you think I think fast enough for you,
tomorrow you will reject me - this is my destiny I
know.

This narrative voice—which can be read as emerging either from the techno-subject or the computer—teases the reader with the bold-faced taunt, **pull the plug why don't you...** If the user clicks on the phrase the program immediately shuts down, throwing her back to the preliminary screen from which the program loads. In this way the work anticipates its own inevitable future when the platform on which it runs is obsolete, and it can no longer be opened. The work at this point will cease to exist, for properly understood, it is not a web site or a CD-ROM—in fact not a product at all—but a series of dynamic processes created when a computer running the appropriate software executes the commands. The work can no more escape its body than its human interlocutors can escape theirs. Whatever future communification holds for us, it will not do away with materiality or the constraints and enablings that materiality entails.

Amidst these complexities, what is clearly established is not the *superiority of code* to flesh but metaphoric networks that map electronic writing onto fluid bodies. *Lexia to Perplexia* intervenes at beginnings and boundaries to tell new stories about how texts and bodies entwine. The shift in materiality that *Lexia to Perplexia* instantiates creates new connections between screen and eye, cursor and hand, computer coding and natural language, space in front of the screen and behind it. Scary and exhilarating, these connections perform human subjects who cannot *be* thought without the intelligent machines that *produce us* even as we produce them.

CHAPTER 5   Experiencing Artists' Books

aye's first encounter with an artist's book was a gift, as was so much in her life, from the Squire of Serendipity. And from her friend Ann Whiston Spirn, who in 1994 had come for a visit and brought as a house gift Johanna Drucker's *Otherspace: Martian Ty/opography*. Kaye loved all books, but she didn't quite know what to make of this one. It did not yield its meanings to her cursory glance through it, and it seemed to have many more images than text, which she perused quickly but did not understand. It would take years and much more experience with experimental WORDIMAGES before she would be prepared to appreciate Drucker's forays into visual typography. Ann explained that artists' books are often produced in small editions, frequently by visual artists, and that they usually come in experimental flavors. But it was not until a couple of years later, when Kaye happened upon Drucker's historical survey *The Century of Artists' Books*, that she began to learn how to read artists' books by reading Drucker. Drucker, both an artist and art historian, gave careful attention to the book's materiality. Her tactful yet penetrating contextualization of the project instantiated by the book, her reading techniques that brought to images many of the same strategies Kaye was accustomed to bringing to words, and most of all her insights into how word and image connected, opened a new world for Kaye. Not since her apprenticeship in graduate school, when the mysteries of the literary text were revealed to her, had she felt a desperate yearning to learn how to read like this. She couldn't imagine why, in a literary education that was fairly extensive, she had never heard of an artist's book, much less handled one.

She had already begun to develop the notion that electronic textuality could be brought into focus by comparing it to print, just as the conventions, materiality, and specificities of print could become more apparent by comparing them to electronic works. She believed that both print and electronic works needed to be taken more seriously as physical artifacts. The biliographers and textual studies scholars were way out in front on this score, developing modes of criticism fully attentive to the book's material properties. But the criticism on

past tense

electronic textuality suffered from an unfortunate divide between computer science folks, who knew how the programs and hardware worked but often had little interest in artistic practices, and literary critics, who too often dealt only with surface effects and not with the underlying processes of the hardware and software. She was looking for a way to talk about hypertext narratives in print and electronic environments that would take the materiality of media into account. She also felt certain there had to be many more print hypertexts than the same tired three or four examples that were usually trotted out, and she suspected she would find them in the tradition of artists' books.

She researched the topic and soon discovered that the Museum of Modern Art in New York City had major holdings, including the famous Furnace Collection. So on her next year's research grant she included a budget for a trip to New York City and Rochester. She remembered from her years as a Rochester undergraduate trudging home in the snow from the bus stop and walking past a building with a small sign, "Visual Studies Workshop." She had often wondered what visual studies might be, a field so remote from her scientific experience that her imagination, which usually revved along at high speed on these walks, failed even to conjure an image. She took the memory to be another prod from Serendipity and resolved to visit it.

The budget did not stretch to cover lodging, so when the time came to make the New York trip, she booked the cheapest hotel she could find over the Internet, reasoning that she meant to spend in the MOMA library every minute it was open, so the hotel didn't matter much anyway. She had gone through the artists' books listed in MOMA's on-line catalogue and whittled her requests down to a hundred, guessing from the descriptions what might be most germane. She was first in line at the door an hour before the library opened, watching New Yorkers scurry by as snow flurries fought for possession of the sidewalk. The scene took her back to her student days—the fleabag hotel, the apple she had bought from a street vendor for lunch—but of course she would not have been able to afford the shockingly high prices of even a fleabag back then. Good, she thought. I am a student again, and I can't wait to get at it. When she was finally ushered into the library, there was a full cart waiting for her and a pair of cotton gloves, which she was instructed to put on before handling the books.

```
N O W
W E E
G E T
O U R
P O E
E M M
A L L
I N N
O N E
R O W
```

She tried to go through them quickly to make a first sort of the most appropriate ones, but they kept seducing her into savoring them, teasing her with their unusual shapes, pop-ups, page textures, complex images, and strategies that made her rethink what a book could be. She lingered over Emmett William's *The VoyAge*. Bound in a simple black cover with white pages over which block letters sail, the book experiments with a digital algorithm by limiting itself to word units comprised of three letters—a constraint that often requires creative spelling—with the spacing between them corresponding to the page numbers on which triads appear. The units on page one are separated by a single space, those on page two, by two spaces, on page fifty, by fifty. Remediating a computer, the page functions as if the spaces are addressable. When the required spacing exceeds the spaces available on the page, the triads drop one-by-one off the page until, as Williams says in his introduction, "after a long solo trip, the last triad vanishes." Moreover, "the frame of each successive page diminishes in size, so that the farther out we go, the harder it is to see the shore, and slowly but surely the poem disappears," making the margins function as if they are a receding shoreline. The content reflects on the constraints of this metric, as on the page that mourns "WOE/WOE/GEO/MET/RIC/FOR/CES/GOB/BLE/UPP/OUR/POE/EMM/BIT/BYE/BIT." The visual patterns formed by the triads make the reader aware of the grid dictating their spacings, invisible in itself but brought into visibility through the dispersed letters. Kaye thought this a wonderful analogy to the underlying code structures of electronic texts, with a similar interplay between the visible surface and the memory addresses in which the bits are stored. In this case, the theme of DISTRIBUTED COGNITION was also in play, although in a different way than with electronic texts. In the poem, the voyage is constituted as an interplay between human agency—the Captain's steering and the narrator's voice that sometimes voices frustration—and the non-human algorithm relentlessly determining how the voyage will proceed.

Michael Snow's *Cover to Cover* provided a fascinating demonstration of how the book can fashion itself as a cybernetic circuit that interpolates the reader's body into its worldview. In this VISUAL NARRATIVE, the first page begins the sequence with a realistic image of a door. On the next page, the image shows a man opening the door to go into a rather ordinary room. With each successive page, the image "opens" the previous representation to reveal it as a posed photograph—for example, by including the photographer in the picture. As Kaye approached the center of the book, the narrative progressed through the house to the street outside, and at the same time the images began shifting angles, becoming obliquely situated on the page. At the book's midpoint she had to turn it upside down to see the remaining images in proper perspective. At the end of *the book she found the* images told a different story when read from back to *front, a shift in* perspective facilitated by the double binding so that *either* cover can function as front. Here, she thought, was a way to create multiple reading paths by making the sequentiality of bound pages function hyptertextually by transforming fundamental properties such as forward and backward, up and down, into relative terms mediated by the orientation of the images and her body's changing position. Moreover, the play with conventions of representation suggested it was impossible to move to a stable exterior frame that would be independent of the inscription apparatus or her physical orientation. Materiality here implied that she was constructed by the book even as she constructed the text through her interactions with it.

don't works / language (in an the same manner

Karen Chance's *Parallax* used similar techniques to construct a hypertextual narrative about two entwined but conflicting perspectives. Using the bright colors of a crayon box, cutouts and a front/back reversal, Chance creates a sequence that from front to back tells the story of a straight man who sees gay men as unwanted intrusions into his life. When she reached the end of the book, Kaye turned it around to go through it backwards, this time reading a visual/verbal narrative about how the same events look from the perspective of a gay man who sees his life threatened by straight people who refuse to acknowledge his existence. The same images, contextualized differently, were made to tell different stories, so that Kaye's physical orientation with respect to the book became an embodied remediation of the two oppositional perspectives embodied in the narrative.

By the third day in the library, her head was bursting with new possibilities opened up by these books, and she raced through the last few so she would have a couple of hours to record her chosen selections with the slide film bought especially for the occasion. She lingered until the last possible moment, finishing the final shot as the library was closing. She emerged into the night to find the air cold and clear, holiday lights shining around her. She paused to let her spinning brain empty itself of thoughts so she could sink into the moment. Everything quieted down, as if even bustling New York were on hold for a second, and out of the moment emerged a thought with quiet clarity. "I'm glad I have lived to see these wonderful books."

The library was closed the next day, her last in the city, so she planned to mosey down to Printed Matter Bookstore, having sussed out that, next to MOMA, it had the best collection of artists' books in town. She liked to rise early, and the bookstore did not open until midmorning, so she treated herself to a walk that ran nearly the length of Manhattan Island from her uptown hotel to Greenwich Village. Run as a collective, Printed Matter began, manager David Platzker explained, when a group of artists realized they had boxes of books stored in their basements that were going to waste. The store has a rule that any artist's book accepted for sale must have a run of at least 100 copies; other than that, anything is game. Kaye spent the day browsing the shelves, and in between customers, David graciously showed her the more expensive items stored in flat files behind the counter. If his generosity in sharing the store's treasures was a sales ploy, it was fantastically successful. By the end of the day Kaye had spent way more money than she intended and walked back wondering how she was going to fit all these books into her suitcase and her budget.

One of her favorite finds was a small hand sewn booklet by Roberta Allen entitled *Pointless Arrows*, with each page decorated by a single vertical line and, on the facing page, an "explanation" of what the line was. As images the lines were all the same, but contextualized by the texts, they all became different. *Spine* by Joan Lyons and Paul Zimmerman used the mirror technique of contextualizing words with images, naming the parts of a book with playful punning images that changed their meanings. The word "leaf," for example, was displayed across an image showing a fall leaf, "flyleaf" with the image of a fly, and so on.

Her trip to the Visual Studies Workshop gave her the opportunity to meet Press Director Joan Lyons, who kindly gave Kaye a tour of the printing facilities at the Workshop. It was Kaye's first encounter with the inscription technology used to produce offset books, and it made a lasting impression. So too did the Workshop's bookstore, where she again found herself unable to resist far too many books. Perhaps the most memorable part of the visit was an observation Lyons made in passing during their conversation. Learning that Kaye was a literary scholar, she remarked that many of the artists' books coming out of the Workshop were more interesting visually than verbally. She speculated this was so because many of the artists tended to locate metaphoric intensity and play in images rather than words. While the images employed a full range of rhetorical devices, including metaphor, simile, pun, condensation, displacement, analogy and inversion, the prose was often rather flat because it was seen as an explanation or amplification of the images. The insight struck home for Kaye, because she recognized that its inverse often held for literary scholars, who tended to locate metaphoric intensity in words and regard images as illustrations of the verbal content. Johanna Drucker was exceptional, Kaye saw, not only for the intelligence and astuteness of her insights but also because she was able to give full weight to both word and image.

Upon her return to California, Kaye found other projects demanding her attention, and it was months before she could pursue the project on her own turf by exploring the splendid artists' book collection at the Getty Research Library.

Universum

She felt privileged to have this magnificent resource a mere ten minutes' drive from her UCLA office, and she felt a joy so intense it approached reverence as she mounted the handsome Travertine marble steps to the main plaza, perched at the top of a mountain, and took in the breathtaking view. She found in the Special Collections room some of the same books she had seen in New York, including "book-like objects," as the Getty catalogue called them, that alluded to books for their conception and significance. Among these was Maurizio Nannucci's *Universum*, a small volume encased in a handsome marbled slipcover. When she removed the cover, Kaye found the book bound on both sides so it could not be opened. Equally playful was Nannucci's *The Medium is Word*, which came in a handsome wood box with a sliding top. Inside was nestled a tan felt bag with a drawstring, and inside that, a black kaleidoscope. When Kaye put it to her eye she saw the black letters "W-O-R-D" along with the usual colored chips. As she turned the tube the letters rolled around to form different patterns, some of them legible as "Word" but many not, forming complex verbal/visual symmetries. Perhaps her favorite book-like object was by Fred A. Hillbruner, according to the catalogue created to "expand catalogers' understanding of the potential range of artists' books." When the object arrived, Kaye found a soft white ball, ten centimeters in diameter, that had the title stamped on it along with the copyright date and the artist's initials. The title said it all: *What is wrong with this book?* It tickled Kaye to see the fifty-cent ball carefully encased in a specially made cardboard box (like those used for all the books in Special Collections) that she estimated must have cost the Getty at least ten dollars to order and purchase. She wondered if the artist had anticipated this irony, speculating that he probably appreciated the joke as much as she did.

That was part of what she loved about the tradition of artists' books. Although some are unique and precious objects, requiring hundreds of hours of meticulous handwork and expensive materials, others are made from castoff materials or humble household items. Her friend Martha Gomez, whom she met during her stay

HTML

INTERFACES

CODE

[illegible]TY

TEXTON

INSCRIPTION TECHNOLOGIES

CREOLE

RHIZOMATIC

VISUAL NARRATIVE / VISUAL LANGUAGE

GLYPHS

MULTIPLE READING PATHS

CHUNKED TEXT

LINKING ME

LINKING MECHANISM

CODEX

RECURSIVE

SAMPLES

MINDBODY

ERGODIC

ORIGINARY SUBJECT

LEXICON LINKMAP / ONTOLOGICAL

SOURCE MATERIAL

AFFORDANCES / REPRESENTATION

ARTIFICIAL LIFE

SPATIAL WRITING

WORD MAPS

UNRELIABLE NARRATOR

To use the Lexicon Linkmap go to
MITPRESS.MIT.EDU/MEDIAWORK

REMEDIATED NARRATOR

SIMULATION

ASSEMBLY CODE

SUBSTRATE

CYBERNETICS

MEDIA-SPECIFIC ANALYSIS

TECHNOTEXTS

SUBJECTIVITY

REMEDIATION

MEDIA

MATERIAL METAPHORS

DIGITAL TECHNOLOGY

ELECTRONIC LITERATURE

FIRST-GENERATION HYPERTEXTS

NONLINEAR

MEDIATION PLOT,

MEDIAL ECOLOGY

REFERENT

EMBODIMENTS

XTML, VRML, DIRECTX,

SECOND-GENERATION ELECTRONIC LITERATURE

HYPERTEXT

CYBERTEXT

MODULAR PROGRAMMING

SIGNIFYING PRACTICES

PROPRIOCEPTION

SIMULACRUM

READER/USER

oks

AND WE SEE THEM
BY SCRATCHING

WITH

SURFACE

OF THE PAGE ON WHICH
THEY
ARE FOUND

at Bellagio on Lake Como, was at work on a book about artists' books produced in Mexico, and she had shown Kaye pictures of books fashioned from used coffee filters, autumn leaves, wooden pencils, and dryer lint. Kaye was entranced with the "can-do" attitude these books implied, as if friends gathered for coffee in the kitchen suddenly turned to each other and said, "Let's make a book!"

While all the books were delightful, her focus on technotexts predisposed her to be blown away by Edwin Schlossberg's *wordswordswords*, a collection of poems written specifically for the material on which each poem is printed. This was a white cotton glove affair, and when she opened the metal box in which the poems lay, she could see why. One of the poems was not inscribed with ink but impressed into sheets of heavy white Italia paper. To read it, Kaye had to slant the papers to catch the light just right; it took her some time to make out the block letter impressions. It spoke of finding the words tactilely by moving one's fingers over the sheet, a soft stroking that correlated with the scratching of one's mind. "Paradox is a way of seeing," another poem entitled "Poem for Jasper" proclaimed from the inked surface of an aluminum sheet, a formulation that the poem went on to characterize as "somewhat true," in a lovely play of self-reflexivity that reminded Kaye of the wariness of generalization instilled in her by scientific training.

Tracing her white-gloved fingers over the rich papers, Kaye thought about the interplay between materiality and mind these beautifully crafted objects initiated. It suddenly struck her that Vannevar Bush was wrong, or at least not entirely right. In his 1945 article "As We May Think," about which we have already heard, Bush argued that his hypertextual machine called the Memex was superior because it worked the way the mind works, through association. Kaye was not sure the claim was correct. Certainly she sometimes caught herself thinking through association, but logical ordering and linear sequencing were also important. Now she was able to clarify her objections. What Bush's formulation neglects, she thought, is the feedback loop from materiality to mind. Obviously artifacts spring from thought, but thought also emerges from interactions with artifacts. Someone starts to make a technical object—a book, say—but in selecting the paper and choosing the cover design, new thoughts come as the materials are handled. Insights are stimulated through touching, seeing, manually fitting parts together, and playing with the materials, that declined to come when the object was merely an abstract proposition. Such breakthroughs appear frequently in science and are almost the norm in creating technological artifacts. They also pepper art history; she thought of Jackson Pollock laying his canvas on the floor, flinging paint on it, and seeing in this action a new potential for making art.

When the MINDBODY is focused on a problem and alert for clues, the material world gives of its bounty unstintingly. Thinking makes shaping, shaping makes thinking, new ideas arrive and are instantiated in more shaping. This was why artists' books were so appealing, Kaye thought, for she saw in them traces of this process. In retracing it, her thoughts too were stimulated and changed by her interaction with the materiality of the artifacts. If books are seen only as immaterial verbal constructs, the rich potential of this interplay is lost. Literary critics have long accepted that form is content and content is form. Now Kaye wanted to shout, "Materiality is content, and content is materiality!" The artists' books had permanently changed her mental landscape—and her senses as well, including vision, tactility, smell, and PROPRIOCEPTION. She would never read books the same way again.

CHAPTER 6   *A Humument* as Technotext: Layered Topographies

Third Edition

A HUMUMENT
A TREATED VICTORIAN NOVEL

TOM PHILLIPS

bones my bones

Among the best known and most beloved artists' books is Tom Phillips's A HUM███████UMENT. Like other works in the genre, A Humument interrogates the material properties of the book and mobilizes them as resources for signification. Its specificity as a technotext comes from its origins in a preexisting book. Intrigued by William Burroughs' cut-ups, Phillips liked the idea of operating on source texts to make entirely new documents. To create A Humument, he took an obscure Victorian novel by William Mallock entitled A Human Document, bought by chance because it met his criterion of costing no more than three pence, and "treated" it by covering over the pages with images that left only a few of the original words visible.

Through curious serendipity, his treatment of Mallock's text reinscribes Mallock's own strategies; Mallock in his "Introduction" creates a persona who agrees to edit a scrapbook of journals, letters, and memorabilia of two recently deceased lovers. These documents are hypertextual, for though "some single thread of narrative, in a feminine handwriting, ran through the whole volume," this was "broken by pages of letters, by scraps of poetry, and various other documents" in a masculine hand (Mallock, p. 4). The editor believes that this profusion of materials disqualifies the scrapbook from being a novel. Uncannily anticipating contemporary descriptions of hypertext narrative, he asserts that "as they stand they are not a story in any literary sense; though they enable us, or rather force us, to construct one out of them for ourselves" (p. 8).

The story that emerges from his recasting of this hypertextual profusion focuses on Grenville, a poet-philosopher turned finance officer, who feels himself on the threshold of a highly successful career in government, complete with a wealthy prospective wife. But before this bright future can materialize, love shakes him around, turning him toward an uncertain future with the unhappily married Irma. The novel attempts to resist its own stultifying conventionality in the editor's positive view of the lovers' illicit liaison—but these resistances, precisely because he regards them as so daring, merely underscore his conservatism.

It is all the more surprising, then, to find in Mallock the postmodern strategy explored by Jennifer A. Wagner-Lawlor in which, she argues, the text shows Irma and Grenville creating their subjectivities through the act of writing. Especially significant for our purposes are scenes of writing where other narrative pathways beckon—for example when Grenville, on looking over his journal, discovers some faint pencil lines he recognizes as a forgotten poem of his. The scene takes place at a moment when he is congratulating himself for being safely beyond love's tumult, the experience described in the poem. With unconscious prescience he decides to ink in the lines, thereby rendering as durable inscription an emotion he will soon experience with life-transforming intensity. It is as if, in hypertext fashion, he is *choosing* by this act of inscription the narrative path he will follow. The trope recurs when Grenville finds in Irma's journal faint writing on the flyleaf, a discovery that reassures him it is their destiny to be lovers. Again possibility is transformed into durable inscription, this time through Grenville's (and behind him, the putative editor's) reinscription of the lines into his journal. These acts of re-writing are repeated twice over on a meta-level: first when the editor surmises that Irma is reinscribing Grenville's journal into her narrative, thus synthesizing their two diaries into a single story, and again by the editor's recasting of Irma's incomplete narrative into the novel he produces from the materials in the scrapbook.

These strategies share a double impulse. On the one hand, they posit precursor texts that embody a hypertextual proliferation of narratives, signified by a diversity of material forms and incomplete or erasable marks. On the other hand, the novel's project is to suppress this unruly complexity, smoothing many conflicting paths into one coherent narrative. This double impulse takes thematic expression through the editor's professed desire to rebel against the "rules" dictating that characters (particularly women) should have only moral thoughts, and his equally strong aversion to the frankness of Zola's *Nana*, which he sees as a moral aberration. His resistance to rules is encoded as the hypertextual proliferation of unruly and multiple narratives, whereas his anxiety about where this might lead is enacted through scenes of writing that over-write previous inscriptions to make them more tractable, predictable, and coherent—which is to say, make them a novel rather than a hypertext.

In "treating" Mallock's novel, Phillips creates an artist's book that seeks to bring into view again this suppressed hypertextual profusion. The opening page proclaims:

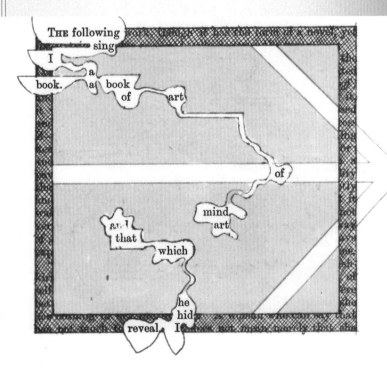

Most of the treatment consists not of coining new words but obliterating ones that already exist, as if to silence the rationalizing consciousness of narrator and editor so that the murmurs of hypertextual resistance to coherent narrative can be heard. Page 178 illustrates the technique; here a page from Mallock's text has been torn, burnt around the edges, and stained in the middle, making most of the text illegible. More typical is page 17, where the few phrases left visible are joined by "rivers" consisting of white spaces between Mallock's words. Visually these rivers of white space trickle down the page, often branching into multiple pathways. Other devices creating hypertextual profusion are leaky borders, which visually separate the page into multiple narrative levels and also transgress this separation, suggesting that distinctions between character, narrator and author are less ontological categories than contingent boundaries susceptible to multiple reconfiguration. Additional hypertextual effects are achieved through interplays between word and image.

All these strategies are on display on page 17, where a central gray rectangle, colored to suggest three-dimensional texture, is placed on a field of variegated yellow, itself centered on another rectangle of variegated tan. The placement of the gray block suggests a page surrounded by margins, which in turn becomes a page in Phillips's text surrounded by the white margins of his book. This arrangement is further complicated by the rivers that run through the borders, as well as by the lexias that extend beyond the outermost yellow field and intrude into the margin's white space, thus suggesting that even the page as Phillips defines it is a boundary to be transgressed. On this page there are several possible sequences in which to read the spatially dispersed words:

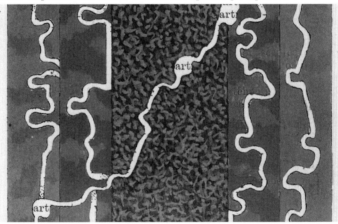

—a repetition that enacts the narrative multiplicity of hypertext and also gently mocks it, since the words are all the same, differing only in their placements within the image. The attentive reader can make out some of Mallock's text through the covering paint, and this effect offers another possible reading sequence.

The text on this page illustrates the nature of the narrative. Broken and reassembled, the prose achieves the compression of poetry, becoming allusive and metaphoric rather than sequentially coherent:

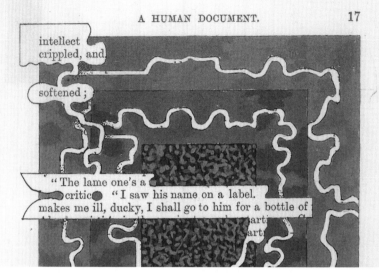

A HUMAN DOCUMENT.   17

intellect
crippled, and

softened ;

" The lame one's a
critic   " I saw his name on a label.
makes me ill, ducky, I shall go to him for a bottle of
art
art

The ambiguity of the hypertextual rivers makes it possible to read these lines as if the <u>REFERENT</u> for "makes me ill" is the critic's name on a label, in which case malady and cure spring from the same source, a bottle of "art/art." Twelve pages earlier comes page 5, which seems to comment on this strategy:

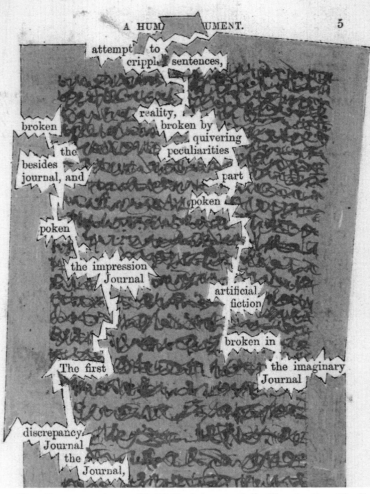

A HUM   UMENT.   5

attempt   to
crippl   sentences,

reality,
broken   broken by
                    quivering
the   peculiarities
besides
journal, and   part

                    poken

poken

      the impression
         Journal

                              artificial
                              fiction

                        broken in

The first   the imaginary
                              Journal

discrepancy
   Journal
      the
         Journal,

Here the comparison with Mallock is especially illuminating. The lines were reworked from the editor's "Introduction," in which he criticizes Irma's style as she strives to make a single narrative out of her diverse materials. Despite himself, the editor admires her "baffled and crippled sentences, her abrupt transitions, and odd lapses of grammar," for though these "could hardly be said to constitute a good description of what she professed to have felt, seemed to be more than that:—they seemed to be a visible witness of its reality, as if her language had been broken by it, like a forest broken by a storm, or as if it were some living tissue, wounded and quivering with sensation" (p. 5).

Yet it is this very hypertextual intensity that the editor smoothes away in his putative recasting. From this smoothed language Phillips, by obliterating most of the editor's words, recovers a sense of the broken language that supposedly underlies it, making the coherent text speak of the "attempt to cripple," a phrase that can be taken to apply to the editor rather than the editor's judgment of Irma's faulty style. Similarly, it is now not Irma's wounded sensations that are "quivering," but the fabric of the perceptual world itself, "reality broken by quivering peculiarities." The strategy of uncovering the putative hypertext underlying Mallock's novel is beautifully captured in "poken," a fractured word that both alludes to the "spoken" of Mallock's text and the evocative, broken language it supposedly covers over.

Contributing to the recovery of hypertextual profusion is the rich interplay between subtext and context, word and image. Running across a visual bend in page 5 are the words:

naming as well as illustrating Phillips' hypertextual breaking of Mallock's page. Also on this page are the squiggly lines that run in rows across the "page" as it is defined by the yellow margins (and then deconstructed as a page by being set within white margins, which recontextualize the page as the leaf in Phillips' text). These squiggles clearly resemble writing—perhaps the handwriting of the journal the editor recasts. Significantly, this writing is illegible as words, transformed into the image or representation of writing rather than writing itself. A similar technique appears on page 83, where the text in the upper right river names:

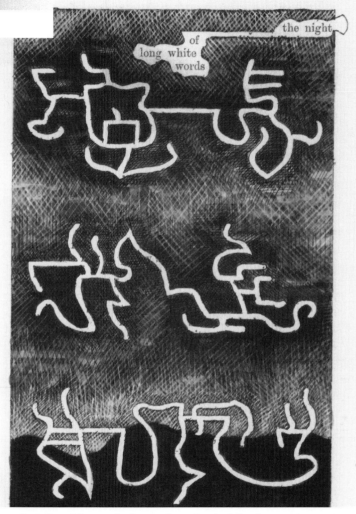

of
long white
words

the night,

a scene that the white squiggles against the dark background seem to enact, although again they are illegible as words and function instead as visual representations of verbal marks. Commenting on this inter-play of word and image in his *Curriculum Vitae* series, Phillips makes an observation equally relevant to *A Humument*: "Once more I empha-size the fact that I regard texts as images in their own right: treated as they are here with words ghosted behind words to form a (literal) sub-text they are all the more image for being doubly text."

Phillips' strategy of recovering and heightening the hypertextual profusion implicit in Mallock's text extends to his own sense that every page offers multiple possibilities for treatment. "In order to prove (to myself) the inexhaustibility of even a single page I started a set of vari-ations on page 85: I have already made over twenty," he comments in the "Notes." So rich does he find Mallock's vocabulary and range of refer-ences that he confesses to using it as his "personal I Ching." He contin-ues to revise *A Humument*, constantly creating new pages that he introduces into subsequent editions and puts up at his web site even before the editions can appear. "If this book finds favour (i.e. sells) and I live," he comments in the Notes, "the consequent reprints will allow me to replace say a dozen pages with each new edition. A notional thirtieth (!) printing therefore would be an entirely reworked book with almost no pages surviving from the first." These remarks suggest that he thinks of Mallock's text as an inexhaustible hypertext, only some of whose possibilities he can actualize in his inscription of narrative pathways, which themselves offer multiple hypertextual readings.

The main character moving through the hypertextual profusion of *A Humument* is Toge, who can appear only on those pages of Mallock's text that contain the words "together" or "altogether," since it is only in these words that the requisite combination of letters making up Toge's name can be found. (Whimsically, Phillips in his "Notes" suggests that Toge's first name is Bill, an extra-textual name that familiarly rein-scribes William Mallock's first name.) In many respects Toge is a typi-cally Romantic character, constantly yearning for Irma, as did Grenville in Mallock's (sub)text. Over and over he finds himself inflated with desire, only to suffer a catastrophic deflation when the erotic liaison

doesn't come off as he hoped. In this reading the narrative is all about **INTERIORIZED SUBJECTIVITY**, which is to say, Toge as an autonomous and independent agent who actualizes himself through the workings of desire. Also in play, however, is his image, which Phillips decided could take shape only through the rivers of white spaces running through Mallock's words. As a result, Toge has an amoeba-like form whose uncertain outlines emerge from the interplay between Mallock's text and Phillips's design. His figure visually testifies to the complication of agency that comes from this union of Phillips with Mallock as his "unwitting collaborator," a production in which Phillips's agency is constrained by Mallock's text, and Mallock's text is transformed in ways the long-deceased writer cannot know, much less control. The processes that inscribe Toge's form as a durable mark embody a multiplication of agency that at the very least complicates, if it does not altogether subvert, his verbal construction as a solitary yearning individual. Page 165 shows

Phillips treating the page by creating backgrounds that make Mallock's text visible through Toge's eyes, mouth, and larynx (body locations associated with perception and articulation), thus literally inscribing Toge as a subject who is spoken as well as a subject who speaks.

A particularly rich interplay between text and image emerges from page 229, a putative photograph of Toge's beloved Irma, doubly framed by a white opaque border and a tan surrounding frame through which the words of Mallock's text are visible, with lines drawn between letters in visual patterns suggestive of hieroglyphics, signifiers based on iconic resemblance.

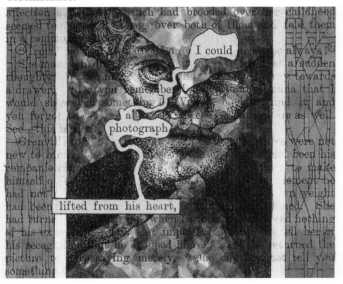

runs a river of text over Irma's face, an articulation that in Romantic fashion locates the image's origin deep inside the interiority of the feeling subject. But an alternate explanation is offered by a river of text that overruns the inset white border and tan hieroglyphics to spill out onto the white border of Phillips' page.

A HUMAN DOCUMENT. 229

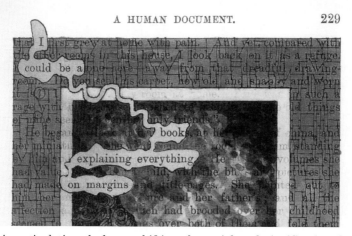

this articulation declares, shifting the weight of signification from image to text and its location from inside the subject to the boundary line between the treated page of Mallock's text and Phillips' own page. On one view voiced on this page, then, art issues from the subject who possesses a consciousness and reaches out into the external world; on another view, it flows into the subject from the external world through interfaces that allow externally originating changes to permeate inward and create the illusion of interiority. At the boundary sit the complexities of the double frames functioning as image and text simultaneously, a double voicing also performed by the text/photograph at the center of these multiple frames.

The interplay between inside and outside, the subject possessing a meaningful interiority and the simultaneous deconstruction of that subject, is strikingly performed on page 150. On this page, Toge steps on the figured carpet and looks through a window at a landscape (the figured carpet and landscape window are so frequently associated with him that Phillips suggests in the "Notes" they function as Toge's two "insignia"). The window through which an artist looks functions as an important motif in Phillips' work as a whole. In *Works and Texts*, critic Huston Paschal points out that Phillips's artist's book *Dante's Inferno* places Dante and Virgil in studies with windows. She writes, "The study/studio bespeaks the artist's dilemma: the creativity that confers a chance for immortality demands a sacrifice. The artist is held hostage to his art."

The rivers of text on page 150 highlight this ambiguity, bracketing Toge's name with two conflicting imperatives to:

150 A HUMAN DOCUMENT.

and to

In commanding Toge to "inspect the landscape," the text evokes it as an actual terrain visible through the window, thus connecting subjectivity with the representation of a world greater than the self. On the other hand, the text also directs Toge to examine the walls "for microscopic incidents," thus alluding to the inward turning that creative in-sight demands. By implication, these conflicting imperatives can be understood as an oscillation between a depth model of realistic representation and a foregrounding of the material means through which such illusions are created, an ambiguity nicely expressed in the juxtaposition of a natural "landscape" with the artificial "fittings."

The oscillation is deepened on the facing page 151. Rendered in colors similar to the landscape Toge "inspects," the image functions visually as a continuation of what Toge sees, as if the authorial eye had moved beyond the window to look at the landscape directly without the mediation of the glass/picture. No sooner has the reader made this transition, however, than the rivers of text recontextualize the landscape as existing in art and memory rather than unmediated perception.

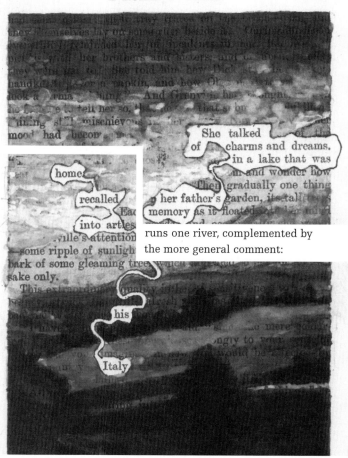

runs one river, complemented by the more general comment:

Whether the landscape emerges from Irma's dreams or Toge's memories of home, it enters the represented world of the text not as an "actual" exteriorized setting it first appeared but as a phantasmatic image that at once confirms the interiority of the subject and subverts it by revealing that interiority as an illusion the flat page creates.

These strategies make us freshly aware that the character is never self-evidently on the page; they also construct Toge as an alter ego for Phillips. As Paschal points out, the alert reader can see signs of Phillips everywhere. On page 44, a scrawl on a brick wall announces "Tom [w]as here," along with the "X" repeated throughout his Terminal Greys series and recurring so frequently in his work that it can be regarded as his "mark." The page forcibly reminds us that Toge exists only insofar as he *is created by* a human author who inscribes durable ink marks on a *flat fiber* surface and a reader who interacts with the book as material object. In *A Humument*, the page is never allowed to disappear by serving only as the portal to an imagined world as it does with realistic fiction. In many ways and on many levels, *A Humument* insists on its materiality.

The material operations of writing and reading take center stage on page 105. This page is visually transformed into the space of the room, inviting us to project our proprioceptive sense into the scene. Moreover, the space is imaged as an art gallery, complete with a picture on the wall and pedestals associated with the display of art objects. Instead of physical objects, here the pedestals are occupied by rivers of text, a move that imaginatively cycles through the (absent) object to arrive at the words. The text reenacts this displacement by proclaiming:

a punningly appropriate phrase that performs what it names, abstracting the missing artifact into "abstract art." The displacement thus cycles through the (representation of) a material object, which gives specificity to the abstract cognitive activity of making these punning connections.

Another pedestal-object proclaims:

while the third comments:

an allusion to the complex processes by which material objects are abstracted into "timeless" art, as if the object could be removed from its historical specificity and treated as a representation that exists independent of its material circumstances.

That this is precisely the move the book resists is suggested by the picture on the wall, which Phillips tells us in the "Notes" was made from pages taken from the first limited edition of *A Humument* by Tetrad Press in 1970. Think of it. First the text exists as a physical object. Then Phillips dismembers the book and rearranges the pages into a material composition that obscures the words and emphasizes the visual qualities of pattern—a process which, if we take him at his word, involved the interplay between thought and artifact as he worked with the pages until he was satisfied with the design. He then used this physical object as the basis for his visual composition, which he inscribed onto Mallock's printed page as a form representing a picture hanging on the wall. When the reader decodes that representation in light of the "Notes," she mentally reconstructs from the flat image the three-dimensional display of crumpled pages, themselves inscribed with words and images Phillips layered onto Mallock's book as he worked with the materiality of the individual pages—a materiality that goes beyond verbal content to include gutters, margins, white space, and the paper fiber as it interacts with paint. In these complex transactions, the artifact (or representation of it) plays an essential role, for it allows the interplay between thought and physicality to craft an emergent materiality ripe with creative potential.

Phillips engaged in a similar process when he pasted pages of *A Humument* over a series of globes, creating visual patterns reminiscent of continents and oceans. Instead of the usual geographical names, phrases from *A Humument* are visible, creating a rich interplay between a material form that gestures toward the world while locating that world within the text's imaginary space. The text-continents, in their simultaneous reference to a fictional world made of words and a (representation of) a world literally made from words, are multilayered collaged compositions that evoke in their complex forms the further complexities of Phillips' images overlaid onto Mallock's text, which remains physically present even in the highly mediated form it takes in this composition, subtly contributing its attraction to the globe's gravitational field.

Complementing these flexible movements between verbal construction and artifactual physicality is the configuration of the page as an interface that implicitly constructs the reader through its materiality. As the two-dimensional page is visually stretched into something like three dimensions, a topographic space is created into which the reader can imaginatively project herself, experiencing the text as a space to explore rather than a line to follow. Because the reader's capability for proprioceptive projection into the text is strengthened, reading is transformed from the subvocalization of interior voices into a more complex activity actualizing the textual space so that it is kinesthetically vibrant as well as verbally resonant. As we have seen, the complex textual layering also has the effect of locating subjectivity ambiguously between a depth model of interiority and the chance juncture of multiple agencies following independent causal lines. As a result, subjectivity for both characters and readers becomes not only a matter of interior voicing but of interaction with a physically evocative world that creates the new precisely because it resists the reduction to an immaterial realm of disembodied verbal signifiers.

Readers are consequently less likely to read the text cover-to-cover than open it at random and mediate over a few pages before skipping elsewhere or closing it for the day. This mode of reading reminds us that in the Middle Ages the codex book was heralded as a great improvement over the scroll precisely because it allowed random reading. In contemporary parlance, we might say that the book is the original random access device (RAD). Contrary to much hype about electronic hypertext, books like *A Humument* allow the reader considerably more freedom of movement and access than do many electronic fictions. In this respect the book is more RAD than most computer texts—a conclusion that the bibliophiles among us will relish.

CHAPTER 7   Embodiments of Material Metaphors

aye was standing in a UCLA gallery, transfixed by an event that all teachers worth their salt dream about— the moment when her students not only surpassed her expectations but leaped ahead of what she herself could have done. She was watching Adriana de Souza e Silva and Fabian Winkler demonstrate their installation *database*. It was their final project for a graduate seminar on word and image in the digital domain, an experimental course she was co-teaching with Bill Seaman, an electronic artist from the Design | Media Arts department. The idea had germinated more than a year earlier, when she and Bill fantasized about a course that would explore the interaction of electronic word, image, sound, and animation. They hoped to combine their complementary expertise to think deeply about the interplay between verbal and nonverbal components in electronic literature and art. Moreover, they strategized about bringing two groups of graduate students into conversation and collaboration with one another: those from literature departments, who excelled in the close reading of difficult texts but often did not have high technical competence or extensive visual skills, and those from Design | Media Arts, who were visually sophisticated and had technical chops but often quailed at reading hundreds of pages of dense theoretical texts. Seminar discussions had been intense, insightful, and rewarding, and the students had caught fire as they planned their final projects.

Adriana and Fabian had taken off on the idea that the materiality of the technology should be brought into visibility, an enterprise they undertook by reversing and subverting its usual operations. The installation consisted of a computer screen displaying virtual text, a printer with a miniature video camera attached, and a projection screen displaying the camera's output. Sitting in the printer were sheets of paper full of text, the exterior database for the project. When the user moves the cursor over the white computer screen, black rectangles appear that cover over most of the text, along with keywords that fade into white again when the cursor moves away—unless the user chooses to click, in which case the keyword is also covered by a black rectangle. At the same time, the click sends a message to the camera to focus on a second keyword in the exterior database related to the first through agonistic relation, perhaps an antonym or some other oppositional tension. For example, clicking on "perpetually" on the screen makes "too fast" appear on the wall projection; the screenic "promise" links to the projected "past." After a few clicks, the screen is dotted with black rectangles. The user can then click on a red dot at the upper right corner to activate a "print" command. The printer sends through the sheet full of pre-written text, blacking out the keywords chosen by the user as the camera gives a fleeting glimpse of them before they disappear. At the same time, the obliterations create alterations in the database's linear narrative text that change its meaning.

Adriana and Fabian's accompanying essay made clear the project's complexity. The inversions bring into visibility a range of assumptions normally so taken for granted they are invisible. The printer obliterates rather than inscribes words; the database is stored as marks on paper rather than binary code inside the computer; clicking blacks out visible words rather than stabilizing them; the camera "reads" but does not record; and the projection displays words oppositional to the ones the user has chosen. The inversions create new sensory, physical, and metaphysical relationships between the user and the database. Printing, a technique normally associated with external memory storage, transforms presence into absence. The video camera, usually linked with storage technologies that make a permanent record, here makes writing ephemeral and transitory, disappearing from the projection as the word is inked out. The database, rather than residing at physically inaccessible sites as bit strings dispersed throughout the hard drive, is here constituted as linear text Kaye could literally hold in her hands.

The significance of these inversions is broadened by the prose constituting the database, selected from various writers meditating on time and memory, including Borges's "The Immortals." In this fiction, the narrator is searching for the City of Immortals. He discovers a tribe of troglodytes, seemingly subhuman creatures that cannot speak, do not sleep, and eat barely enough to keep alive. The narrator decides to teach one of them to speak, only to discover that the creature is the poet Homer. Following Borges's logic, Adriana and Fabian point out that immortality drastically alters one's relationship to time. Since time for an

immortal stretches in an endless horizon, the future ceases to have meaning; the future is precious for mortals because they understand their lives have finite horizons. The immortals, by contrast, live in a present that obliterates the past and devours the future, becoming absolute, permanent, and infinite. Saturated by memories stretching into infinity, the immortals become incapable of action, paralyzed by thoughts that have accumulated through eons without erasure. Seen in light of this story, the obliterations the printer creates can be read as inscriptions of mortality, non-signifying marks that paradoxically signify the ability to forget, a capability the immortals do not have.

Just as the printer plays with time by linking inscribing/obliterating with immortality/mortality, so the wall projection plays with time by linking writing/ speaking with visibility/invisibility. The words projected on the wall function as visible inscriptions, but inscriptions that behave like speaking since they disappear as the printer inks out the selected word. Writing, a technology invented to preserve speech from temporal decay, here is made to instantiate the very ephemerality it was designed to resist. Kaye understood that her relation to this writing was being reconfigured to require the same mode of attention she normally gave to speech. If her thoughts wandered and her attention lapsed while she was listening to someone speak, it was impossible to go back and recover what was lost, in contrast to rereading a passage in a book. Moreover, the wall projection did not repeat the word she selected on screen but rather substituted another word orthogonally related to it. Blacked out as soon as she clicked on it, the screen word became unavailable to visual inspection. She could "remember" it only by attempting to triangulate on it using the projected word, which required her to negotiate a relationship constructed by someone else through the fields of meaning contained in the database. But as soon as she printed the database out, it was altered by the printer obliterating the words she had selected, which also changed the meaning of the narrative that provided the basis for the relationship between screenic and projected words. Thus she was placed in the position of trying to negotiate meanings whose significances were changed by her attempt to understand them. Cagey, she thought, very cagey. Not to mention a stunning interrogation of the assumptions that underlie our acts of reading and writing.

What does it mean to "do" theory? As practiced in the sciences, theory distills from experience a few underlying regularities, thus reducing a seemingly infinite number of particularities into a parsimonious few. The more instances that can be reduced, the more powerful the theory is understood to be. Because the noise of reality cannot be so easily tamed, scientific theories always exist in tension with experimental data. Deviation from theoretically predicted results is the mark of the real, the inscription of interacting complexities that may rarely or never be completely eliminated. The point of experimental practice is to reduce this noise as much as possible. Reduction is good, proliferation is bad.

Theory in literature has related meanings but different cumulative effects. Here theory serves as an interpretive framework through which particular instances of literary texts can be read. Like scientific experiments, texts may rarely or never be completely explained by a given theory; there will always be elements that resist incorporation into a theoretical matrix. Unlike scientific theory, however, the more predictive power a literary theory seems to have, in which it yields readings that can be known in advance once the theory is specified, the less valuable it becomes. At this point literary scholars tend to feel the theory has become reductive in a bad sense, because it represses the text's power to generate new meanings and so to renew itself. Here reduction is bad, proliferation good.

Years ago I proposed an economic interpretation for this difference, suggesting that whereas science can renew itself by continually opening new realms of phenomena for investigation, literature is in the very different position of having an established canon of a finite number of texts. While some new frontiers can be opened by expanding the canon or, in the case of contemporary literature, adding to it through new works, it is unlikely that there will ever be new plays by Shakespeare or new medieval texts to study. "Too many critics, too few texts" was the way I expressed this situation, leading to a dynamic in which the economics require that old texts must be capable of being read in new ways if literary scholars are to publish new research. The inexhaustibility of texts thus comes to have an economic value very different from the noise of experimentation in science. Rather than trying to eradicate noise, literary scholars have a vested interest in preserving it. When literary theories become sufficiently established that they threaten to make this noise invisible, they cease to have the same utility for critics and will normally be employed in different ways. They are then less likely to be seen as interpretive frameworks dictating entire readings than to be regarded as one tool among many, used for discrete passages or momentary insights but rarely the central focus of a critical argument. Literary theories thus have life cycles distinctively different from that of scientific theories (itself a complex topic too extensive to discuss here).

In addition, the ideology of science sees theories as cumulative (or more precisely, subsumptive). Older established theories, for example Newton's laws of motion, must be reconciled with newer theories and folded into them, as when mechanics is established as a limit case to quantum mechanics. Although it is a moot point whether this is a smooth folding or a rupture covered over by changing what key terms mean, nevertheless it is fair to say that the cumulative effect of theory building is greater in science than in literature. This difference too gives literary theories sharper and more well-defined life cycles than scientific theories.

Anecdotal evidence has a shifting value for literary theory that varies according to where in the life cycle it comes. Particularity weighs in most heavily at the beginning of theory formation, when it gives vividness and heft to theory's generalizations, and near the end of the cycle, when it often serves to unravel a theory or force it to reorganize at a higher level of complexity. At the moment, we are near the beginning of a theory of media-specific analysis in literary studies. Many people, Kaye thought, are now making journeys similar to hers, moving from print-oriented perspectives to frameworks that implicitly require the comparison of electronic textuality and print to clarify the specificities of each. Others have yet to begin the trip, remaining firmly within print and seeing electronic textuality as a subset of print or as something still too distant to be an important consideration. For these folks, theory might provide the best catalyst for re-thinking their perspective, since they do not yet have the experiences that would make electronic textuality an everyday part of their lives. Theory, with generalizations distilled from personal encounters with texts, can stimulate scholars to read old texts in new ways and seek out new texts that cannot be adequately understood without the theory. Maybe now is a good time for a double-braided text where the generalities of theory and the particularities of personal experience can both speak, though necessarily in different voices. A text where both voices can be heard, at first very different but then gradually coming closer until finally they are indistinguishable.

Just as image and text, materiality and content, have entwined both in the narrative and theoretical chapters, so now the two voices of personal experience and theoretical argument merge as Kaye's cumulative experience leads her to the theoretical concepts articulated at the start of this book. The end is in the beginning, and the beginning is in the end. Kaye's laboratory experiences, her first disciplined encounter with materiality, no doubt predisposed her to realize that books are more than encoded voices; they are also physical artifacts whose material properties offer potent resources for creating meaning. Indeed, it is impossible not to create meaning through a work's materiality. Even when the interface is rendered as transparent as possible, this very immediacy is itself an act of meaning-making that positions the reader in a specific material relationship with the imaginative world evoked by the text.

The ~~database~~ project makes this unmistakably clear by positioning the database of verbal signifiers within a complex semiotic-material apparatus that integrates the words with a series of machine interfaces that materially affect their meaning. Moreover, through its rigorous interrogation of the ways in which users interact with the interfaces, it also makes clear that subjectivity is an emergent property produced in part by the work's materiality. The interplay between semiotic components and physical attributes that gives rise to materiality simultaneously and with the same gesture gives rise to subjects who both perceive and are acted upon by this materiality.

In the broadest sense, artistic practice can be understood as the crafting of materiality so as to produce human-intelligible meanings, while at the same time transforming the meaning of terms like "human" and "intelligible." A critical practice that ignores materiality, or that reduces it to a narrow range of engagements, cuts itself off from the exuberant possibilities of all the unpredictable things that happen when we as embodied creatures interact with the rich physicality of the world. Literature was never only words, never merely immaterial verbal constructions. Literary texts, like us, have bodies, an actuality necessitating that their materialities and meanings are deeply interwoven into each other.

CHAPTER 8   Inhabiting *House of Leaves*

SE OF LEAVES

Z. DANIELEWSKI

A Novel

I
f my case for the importance of materiality rested only on *A Humument* and *Lexia to Perplexia*, it might risk being seen as special pleading; for these texts, wonderful though they are, are somewhat anomalous in the literary tradition. *House of Leaves* demonstrates that materialist strategies are also intimately involved in a best-selling novel. Camouflaged as a haunted house tale, *House of Leaves* is a metaphysical inquiry worlds away from the likes of *The Amityville Horror*. It instantiates the crisis characteristic of post-modernism, in which representation is short-circuited by the realization that there is no reality independent of mediation. The book does not try to penetrate through cultural constructions to reach an original object of inquiry—an impossible task. On the contrary, it uses the very multi-layered inscriptions that create the book as a physical artifact to imagine the subject as a palimpsest, emerging not behind but *through* the inscriptions that bring the book into being.

The book's putative subject is the film *The Navidson Record*, produced by the world-famous photographer Will Navidson after he, his partner Karen Green, and their two children Chad and Daisy occupy the House of Ashtree Lane in a move intended to strengthen their strained relationships and knit them closer as a family. Precisely the opposite happens when the House is revealed as a shifting labyrinth of enormous proportions, leading to the horrors recorded on the high-8 videos Will installed throughout the house to memorialize their move. From this video footage he made *The Navidson Record*, which then becomes the subject of an extensive commentary by the solitary Zampanò. When the old man is discovered dead in his apartment, the trunk containing his notes, scribblings, and speculations is inherited by the twenty-something Johnny Truant, who sets about ordering them into a narrative to which he appends his own footnotes, which in *Pale Fire* fashion balloon into a competing/complementary narrative of its own. Zampanò's narrative, set in the typeface Times, occupies the upper portion of the pages while Johnny's footnotes live below the line in Courier, but this initial ordering becomes increasingly complex as the book proceeds.

Equally complex is the ontological status of objects represented within the book and finally the materiality of the book itself. In his introduction, Johnny Truant reveals that the film *The Navidson Record*, about which he, Zampanò and others write thousands of pages, may in fact be a hoax:

> After all, as I fast discovered, Zampanò's entire project is about a film which doesn't even exist. You can look, I have, but no matter how long you search you will never find The Navidson Record in

xix

> theaters or video stores. Furthermore, most of what's said by famous people has been made up. I tried contacting all of them. Those that took the time to respond told me they had never heard of Will Navidson let alone Zampanò.

(p. xix-xx). Yet as the many pages that follow testify, the lack of a real world referent does not result in mere absence. Zampanò's account contains allusions, citations and analyses of hundreds of interpretations of *The Navidson Record*, along with hundreds more ancillary texts. Johnny Truant's footnotes, parasitically attaching themselves to Zampanò's host narrative, are parasited in turn by footnotes written by the anonymous "Editors," upon which are hyper-parasitically fastened the materials in the Exhibits, Appendix, and finally the Index (which like the index of *Pale Fire* turns out to be an encrypted pseudo-narrative of its own).

To make matters worse (or better), this proliferation of words happens in the represented world on astonishingly diverse media that match in variety and strangeness the sources from which the words come. The inscription technologies include film, video, photography, tattoos, typewriters, telegraphy, handwriting, and digital computers. The inscription surfaces are no less varied, as Johnny Truant observes about Zampanò's notes, including writing on **old napkins, the tattered edges of an envelope, once even on the back of a postage stamp; everything and anything but empty; eac fragment completely covered with the creep of years and years of ink pronouncements; layered, crossed out amended; handwritten, typed; legible, illegible; impenetrable, lucid; torn, stained, scotch taped; som bits crisp and clean, others faded, burnt or folded and refolded so many times the creases have obliterated whole passages of god knows what—sense? truth? deceit?** (p. xvii). Despite his uncertainty (or perhaps because of it), he adds to these "snarls" by more obsessive writing on diverse surfaces, annotating, correcting, recovering, blotting out and amending Zampanò's words, filling out a journal, penning letters and poems, even scribbling on the walls of his studio apartment until all available inscription surfaces are written and over-written with more words and images.

None of the dynamics displayed in *House of Leaves* is entirely original, yet the bits and pieces add up to something very specific if not unique. What distinguishes *House of Leaves* is the way it uses familiar techniques to accomplish two goals. First, it extends the claims of the print book by showing what print can be in a digital age; second, it recuperates the vitality of the novel as a genre by recovering, *through the processes of remediation themselves*, subjectivities coherent enough to become the foci of the sustained narration that remains the hallmark of the print novel. The computer has often been proclaimed the ultimate medium because it can incorporate every other medium within itself. As if imitating the computer's omnivorous appetite, *House of Leaves* in a frenzy of remediation attempts to eat all the other media, but this binging leaves traces on the text's body, resulting in a transformed physical and narrative corpus. In a sense House of Leaves recuperates the traditions of the print book and particularly the novel as a literary form, but the price it pays for this recuperation is a metamorphosis so profound it becomes a new kind of form and artifact. It is an open question whether this transformation represents the rebirth of the novel, or the beginning of the novel's displacement by a hybrid discourse that as yet has no name.

These transformative processes are on display in an early scene between Will Navidson and Karen Green. The scene is related by Zampanò, who positions his readers as first-person viewers watching the film of *The Navidson Record* along with him. Since the film does not exist, his description, which inevitably interprets as well as a remediates, creates the film as an object within the text and also as a putative object in the represented world. He describes how Navidson takes Karen's jewelry box out of a crate and removes the lid and inner tray to look inside, although

Unfortunately, whatever he sees inside is invisible to the camera. (p. 10). Later we learn that Karen keeps old love letters in her jewelry box, so the moment is fraught with an invasion of her privacy and an implicit jealousy by Navidson. Then Karen comes in as Navidson is pulling a clump of her hair from her hairbrush; she watches as he tosses it into the waste-basket. She tries to snatch the hair, saying, "Just you watch, one day I'll go bald, then won't you be sorry you threw that away." "No," Navidson replies with a grin.

Zampanò's commentary focuses on the multiple ways in which these few seconds demonstrate how much Navidson values Karen. Despite the casual way Will handles her things, Zampanò's interpretation claims that Navidson has in effect preserved her hair, called into question his own behavior through the way he edits the images, thus contrasting his attitude at the time he edited the video with his apparent disregard for her privacy at the time the high-8 camera caught his actions.

The layering here is already four-fold, moving from Navidson and Karen at the time of filming, through Navidson as he edits the film, to Zampanò's initial viewing of the film, to his re-creation of the scene for us, the putative viewers, who of course read words rather than see images and so add a fifth layer of mediation. The layering is further complicated when Zampanò introduces "Samuel T. Glade," a critic who points out the ambi-guity of Navidson's "No," arguing that it could refer to either "watch," "bald," or "sorry" or all three. (p. 11). As the meanings proliferate, Navidson's relationship with Karen became similarly multilayered and complex, combining disregard with tenderness, jealousy with regret, playful resistance to her chiding with a deep wish to recover what he has thrown away. But these complexities all come from the multiple remediations of the supposedly original moment, recorded on a film that does not exist in a house that cannot be because it violates the fundamental laws of physics. Thus subjects (in this case Will, Karen, and their relationship) are evacuated as originary objects of representation but reconstituted through multiple layers of remediation.

The pattern is repeated throughout the text. When relationships are not mediated by inscription technologies they decay toward alienation, and when they are mediated, they progress toward intimacy. Karen's distrust of Will grows as he becomes increasingly infatuated with exploring the House, and only when she makes a film about him, "A Brief History of Who I Love," can she see him with fresh eyes and rekindle her love. Here is Zampanò's interpretation of the process:

The diligence, discipline, and time-consuming research required t fashion this short—there are easily over a hundred edits—allowed Kare for the first time to see Navidson as something other than her own person fears and projections. (p. 368). Navidson undergoes a similar process when he makes "Tom's Story," his edited version of the videotape recording his brother Tom while Will forges ahead to explore the House. When Navidson returns, he finds that Tom has left his post and bitterly complains: "This is Tom. This is what Tom does best. He lets you down." (p. 277). Only in retrospect, after he edits the tape following Tom's death, does Navidson recapture their childhood closeness and recuperate a far more loving vision of Tom. Zampanò, calling the edited tape:

a labor of love, a set piece sibling to Karen's short
film on Navidson.   stresses there is

nothing hasty about Tom's Story. Navidson has
clearly put an enormous amount of work into these few
nutes. Despite obvious technological limitations, the cuts
clean and sound beautifully balanced with the rhythm and
ler of every shot only serving to intensify even the most
ordinary moment.   ...

f Sorrow is *deep regret over someone loved,* there is
thing but regret here, as if Navidson with his great eye
ad for the first time seen what over the years he never
should have missed.   (p. 274).

Although we can tease out a temporal sequence for the events represented in *The Navidson Record*, these actions are screened through a complex
temporality of remediation. The <u>MEDIATION PLOT</u>, if I may call it that, proceeds from the narration of the film as a representation of events, to the
narration of the film as an artifact in which editing transforms meaning, to
the narration of different critical views about the film, to Zampanò's narration as he often disagrees with and re-interprets these interpretations, and
finally to Johnny's commentary on Zampanò's narration. Onto this already
complex pastiche is layered a related but distinct temporality constituted
by the different processes of inscription. This sequence begins with articles
and books that Zampanò collects and reinscribes in his commentary, proceeds to Johnny's writing as he orders Zampanò's notes into a manuscript,
and supposedly ends with the editors' emendations and publisher's inter-
ventions as they convert the manuscript to a print book. Onto the chronol-
ogy of events and the order of telling are thus overlaid further temporal
complexities introduced by recognizing that the narration is not an oral
production but a palimpsest of inscriptions on diverse media. Consequently, the story's architecture is envisioned not so much as a sequential
narrative as alternative paths within the same immense labyrinth of a fictional spacetime that is also and simultaneously a rat's nest of inscription

surfaces that prove to be as resistant to logical ordering as the House is to coherent mapping. Locating itself within these labyrinthine spaces, the text enfolds the objects represented together with the media used to represent them, thus making itself into a material metaphor for the recursive complexities of contemporary medial ecology.

At the same time, *House of Leaves* insists on its specificity as a print novel, showing a heightened self-awareness about its own materiality. To see this self-consciousness at work, compare the narrative strategies of *House of Leaves* with those of the turn-of-the-century novel as it began to move away from realism and into stream-of-consciousness. Think of the moment in *Heart of Darkness* when Marlow sits on the deck of the *Nellie* and spins his tale. It is a critical truism that Marlow's consciousness creates multiple layers within the narration. His account of Kurtz's death to the Intended differs from his narration of that moment to the men on the ship, both of which can be supposed to differ, subtly or substantially, from how he would relate it to himself. But there is no recognition in the text of how these multiple oral narrations are transcribed into writing. However visible the mediations of consciousness (and unconsciousness), the technologies of inscription are invisible, their effects erased from the narrative world. Moreover, there is no consideration of how mastery of technique (or lack of it) might affect the inscriptions, whereas *House of Leaves* offers extended reflections on how Navidson's "great eye" affects the film Zampanò narrates.

In *Heart of Darkness* events are never seen apart from mediating consciousness; in *House of Leaves* consciousness is never seen apart from mediating inscription devices. The text emphasizes that people within the represented world—Will Navidson and Karen Green on one level, Zampanò on another, and Johnny Truant on yet another—exist only because they have been recorded. Moreover, these characters participate in further cycles of remediation as they use inscription technologies to explore past trauma, reenvision relationships that have been damaged, and understand the relation of themselves and others to the inscriptions that bring them into being. The UNRELIABLE NARRATOR, a literary invention foregrounding the role of consciousness in constructing reality, has here given way to the

REMEDIATED NARRATOR, a literary invention foregrounding a proliferation of inscription technologies that evacuate consciousness as the source of production and recover in its place a mediated subjectivity that cannot be conceived as an independent entity. Consciousness alone is no longer the relevant frame but rather consciousness fused with technologies of inscription.

It is not difficult to hear in some of Zampanò's remarks the views of the author as he draws attention to this fusion. Consider Zampanò's comments at the conclusion of the breathless narration in which the house eats Tom, a point where the action explodes and we are allowed for a moment to forget the layers of mediation separating us from the putative event. This momentary lapse into pseudo-realistic narration ends as soon as the climactic sequence is over, when footnote 308 reminds us that:

the chaotic bits of tape representing these
must be supplemented with Billy's narration.
Zampanò emphasizes that Navidson   makes Reston the sequence's sole authority. This is
pecially since Reston saw none of it. He is only recounting what Navidson told him himself. The
consensus has always been that the memory is simply too painful for Navidson to revisit. But there
ner possibility: Navidson refuses to abandon the more perspicacious portion of his audience. By
on Reston as the sole narrative voice, he subtly draws attention once again to the question of
acies in representation, no matter the medium, no matter how flawless. Here in particular, he
gly emphasizes the fallen nature of any history by purposefully concocting an absurd number
rations. Consider: 1. Tom's broken hands ──────▶ 2. Navidson's perception of Tom's hurt
────▶ 3. Navidson's description of Tom's hurt to Reston ──────▶ 4. Reston's re-telling of
on's description based on Navidson's recollection and perception of Tom's actual hurt. A pointed
er that representation does not replace. It only offers distance and in rare cases perspective.

346

The "pointed reminder" sharpens when we discover that the Last Interview is missing, so that we see the complex chain of mediation *only* through Zampanò's written remediation of it, remediated in turn by Johnny and the editors.

So intricate are the layers of mediation that unmediated moments are glaring in their incongruity once we notice them. Commenting upon how obsessed Navidson is with the house prior to his final exploration, Zampanò delivers the following account meant to show that Navidson has become deadened to stimuli that ordinarily would arouse intense emotions. The scene begins **back in October when Navidson first came across the tape of Wax kissing Karen** a sequence we have already read in another context. The point in Zampanò's re-telling of the scene is that Navidson **hardly responded. He viewed the scene twice, once at regular speed, the second time on fast forward, and then moved on to the rest of the footage without saying a word.** (p. 397). If we have our wits about us we may ask, how can Zampanò possibly know how Navidson viewed this scene? There is no possibility he was actually in the room, so he could know only if Navidson recounted his reaction in the missing Last Interview, about which nothing is said in the text, or made a tape of himself editing the tape. But the tape of Navidson watching the tape would itself have been subject to editing, cuts, and other manipulations, so it could not function as a naive record but only as another interpretation. Moreover, Zampanò's comments come not from his own viewing or reading but from his analysis of the Haven-Slocum Theory (HST). In the view of the HST, Navidson's lack of reaction becomes "highly climactic" precisely because it is an absence where there should have been a presence. **The pain anyone else would have felt while viewing that screen kiss, in Navidson's case has been blunted by the grossly disproportionate trauma already caused by the house. In this regard it is in fact a highly climactic, if irregular moment only because it is so disturbing to watch something so typically meaningful rendered so utterly inconsequential.** (p. 397). The negative thrust of the argument is sufficiently convoluted that it may almost succeed in keeping us from noticing there is no way the putative object of inquiry—Navidson watching the tape of the kiss—could have been observed by those who interpret it. This incongruity, a mediated version of what film-makers call a continuity error, creates an absence at the center of the presence manufactured by the multiple layers of interpretation. The interpretation exists, in fact several layers of interpretation, but the real-world object is as impossible to conjure up the House on Ash Tree Lane, an impossible object because its interior dimensions exceed its exterior measurements.

Mark Johnson and George Lakoff have written about the elemental schema that express themselves in "metaphors we live by," so pervasive and fundamental they often are not even recognized as metaphors. Among these schema are inside/outside and container/contained. We assume, without thinking much about it, that the inside must be smaller than the outside that encases it, and the contained must be smaller than the container if only by the thickness of the walls. Violating these preconscious assumptions, the impossible House nevertheless enters the space of representation, much like M. C. Escher's ascending/descending staircases (references to Escher's self-deconstructing spaces pepper the *House*'s footnotes). The House is undeniably present within the text, yet in crucial aspects it remains unrepresentable. The interior hallway that mysteriously creates a door in the living room where there was none before leads to spaces, supposedly contained by the dimensions of an ordinary two-bedroom family house, greater than the diameter of the earth and older than the solar system.

The absence at the center of this space is not merely nothing. Rather, it is so commanding and absolute that it paradoxically becomes an especially intense kind of presence, violent in its impossibility and impossible to ignore. Navidson, insisting that his documentary should be taken literally, is quoted by Zampanò as saying:

And if one day you find yourself passing by that house, don't stop, don't slow down, just keep going. There's nothing there. Beware."

(p. 4). Only if we read "nothing" as a substantive does this passage make sense, a negation converted into the looming threat of something, although it is impossible to say what unless it be negation itself, working to obliterate our everyday assumptions about reality.

One of the tropes for this threat is the beast that manifests itself through physical traces that always remain shy of verifiable presence. So we read about the mysterious claw marks of some enormous paw that Johnny finds alongside Zampanò's dead body; the deep growls that issue from the House, untraceable traces that may be the sound of the beast or perhaps just the House groaning in its endless rearrangements; the rending of the fluorescent markers with which the explorers try to map the House's interior, along with the destruction of their supplies; the rank odor that Johnny first encounters in Zampanò's apartment and that he identifies then with the smell of history; the ominous creatures that populate the margins of Chad and Daisy's classroom drawings, with the intense black square in the middle that grows larger in each painting; the black hand of darkness that swipes into the camera frame to consume Holloway's dead body. Representing both the interiority of psychological trauma and the exteriority of raging appetite, the beast, like the House itself, inhabits a borderland between the metaphoric and the literal, the imaginary and the real.

Nowhere is the dance between presence and absence more deftly executed than in the scene where Johnny goes into the storeroom at the tattoo shop to load up a tray with ink. As the door swings shut behind him, he suddenly senses that something is going "extremely wrong" and thinks he sees the beast's eyes "full of blood." The narration from this point on is full of contradictions. He smells a stench and we may believe it is the rank smell of the beast until Johnny confesses:

I've shit myself. Pissed myself too. Increasingly incoherent, he sees **The shape of a shape of a shape of a face dis(as)sembling before my eyes.** (p.71). He bolts from the storeroom through a door that is inexplicably open rather than shut and tumbles down the stairs as **Something hisses slashes out at the back of my neck.** Although a client in the shop later calls Johnny's attention to the "long, bloody scratch" on the back of his neck, other details he reported come undone in the continuing narration. He discovers, for example, that he has not soiled his pants after all. Moreover, the scratch that remains the only verifiable evidence of the

144Not only are there no hot-air registers, return air vents, or radiators, cast iron or other, or cooling systems—condenser, reheat coils, heating convector, damper, concentrator, dilute solution, heat exchanger, absorber, evaporator, solution pump, evaporator recirculating pump—or any type of ducts, whether spiral lock-seam/standing rib design, double-wall duct, and Loloss^TM Tee, flat oval, or round duct with perforated inner liner, insulation, and outer shell; no HVAC system at all, even a crude air distribution system—there are no windows—no water supplies,

encounter recalls the half-moon cuts his mother left on his neck when she tried to strangle him at age seven. Is the triply mediated "shape of a shape of a shape of a face" the face of the beast, or of the mother who herself remains an incomprehensible object for Johnny in the intensity of her love equaled only by the ferocity of her insanity and abuse?

The ambiguities already inscribed into the scene intensify when Johnny looks down at his body covered by ink spilled in his mad dash down the stairs and sees it as an "omen." I'm doused in black ink, my hands completely covered, and see the floor is black, and—have you cipated this or should I be more explicit?—jet on jet; for a ding instant I have watched my hand vanish, in fact all of me has shed, one hell of a disappearing act too, the already foreseen olution of the self, lost without contrast, slipping into oblivion,

At this point the "foreseen" dissolution of his identity connects with the beast as a signifier of absence, a negation that spreads like an inkblot to encompass his subjectivity. But then the passage continues by recovering, through a doubly mediated reflection, the blotted-out subject:

l mid-gasp I catch sight of my reflection in the back of the tray, ghost in the way: seems I'm not gone, not quite. My face has been ttered with purple, as have my arms, granting contrast, and thus ning me, marking me, and at least for the moment, preserving me.

(p. 72). The purple ink that brings back portions of his splattered face recalls the purple nail polish his mother wore the day her fingernails dug into his neck, marking him in a complex act of inscription that here merges

144Not only are there no hot-air registers, return air vents, or radiators, cast iron or other, or cooling systems—condenser, reheat coils, heating convector, damper, concentrator, dilute solution, heat exchanger, absorber, evaporator, solution pump, evaporator recirculating pump—or any type of ducts, whether spiral lock-seam\standing rib design, double-wall duct, and Loloss™ Tee, flat oval, or round duct with perforated inner liner, insulation, and outer shell; no HVAC system at all, even a crude air distribution system—there are no windows—no water supplies,

with the purple and black ink to form an over-determined double writing that operates simultaneously to negate and assert, obliterate and create, erase and mark.

The play between presence and absence is extended through the dynamic interplay between words and non-verbal signifying practices. The effects achieved by *House of Leaves* through this dynamic interplay are specific to the print book; they could not operate the same way in any other medium.

Consider for example the unusual typography of Chapter IX, where there is a wide diversity of typefaces and spatial orientations, with the type set so that it goes in many directions including upside down, sideways and in reverse. Zampanò suggests this chapter should be called "The Labyrinth," a title that makes explicit what is already implicit in the typography, that *House of Leaves* mirrors the House on Ashtree Lane, both of which are figured as a labyrinth, a motif also embossed in black-on-black on the cover.

The analogy between the labyrinthine physical form of Chapter IX and the House can be traced through footnote 144 (p. 119). This extremely odd annotation perches near the top of the page inside a box outlined with a blue line, a significant hue because it is the color used for the word "House," which appears in blue throughout the text, including equivalent words in languages other than English (haus, casa, etc.). The footnote is attached to a passage in which Zampanò remarks upon the utter nkness found within the House's mysterious interior:

Nothing there provides a reason to linger. In part ause not one object, let alone fixture or other manner of finish work has r been discovered there.[144] (p. 119). Despite Zampanò's comment that we should not linger, footnote 144 attempts to enumerate over the space of twenty-five pages everything that is *not* in the House, from hot-air registers and bathtubs to a Christmas tree. Since nothing is in the House, the list of what is absent, even if limited to accoutrements usually found in houses, is infinite. If we read the blue color as an evocation of the blue screen of a movie backdrop onto which anything can be projected, then the text is attempting to project into this space the linguistic signifiers for everything in the world, as if attempting to make up through verbal proliferation the absolute emptiness of the House as a physical space.

Moreover, the type is set so that when we turn the page over, the words inside the blue box are repeated from the other side but in reverse, as if we were seeing them from the inside of a barbershop window decorated with text meant to be read from the outside. The box calls into question an assumption so commonplace we are not normally aware of it—that book pages are opaque, a property that defines one page as separate from another. Here the back of the page seems to open transparently onto the front, a notion that overruns the boundary between them and constructs the page as a leaky container rather than an unambiguous unit of print. Treating the page as a window can be seen as a way to compensate for the House's viewless interior. After denying us any transparency through which we can look into or out of the House, the text turns its own material substrate into a window that proposes to bring into view everything *not* in the house, an enterprise as paradoxical as it is quixotic.

Even after the words cease, the box in which they were inscribed continues to signify. It next appears bereft of words but filled with light blue color, as if it has once again become the blue screen of film production. The reverse of this page shows the box filled in with black ink, an image that suggests either nothingness or inscriptions so densely over-written they have obliterated themselves. The facing page shows only a blank space where the box has been, its defining blue border erased along with the text. Thus the fullness of an ink-black square is linked with nothingness, the blue screen of infinite malleability with the articulation of an infinite series, the opaque front of a page with a transparent back. The dynamic interplay between words, nonverbal marks, and physical properties of the page work together to construct the book's materiality so that it functions as a mirror to the mysterious House, reversing, reflecting and inverting its characteristics even as it foregrounds its own role as a container for the fictional universe in which such an impossible object could exist.

Larry McCafferey, a colleague who teaches at San Diego State University, is a force of nature, a white-haired wiry dynamo who has made himself an expert on the Anza Borrega desert area where he lives. Since we both work on contemporary American literature, we had come to know and like one another. Late one afternoon he called to explain he had set up a meeting with Mark Danielewski but was having second thoughts because he was scheduled for a strenuous mountain climb early the next morning, and he invited me to go in his place. I jumped at the chance. I was told the bar was in Santa Monica, an easy half-hour drive from my house. When I began cruising down Santa Monica Boulevard in the death-defying Friday night traffic, I realized the bar is in fact in West Hollywood, a trendy area inaccessible by any major freeway. So I had no choice but to continue my grueling course down Santa Monica, taking on stoplight-by-stoplight the Jaguars, Mustangs and other fauna native to these streets. I arrived an hour-and-a-half late, but mercifully Mark was willing to forgive me and even to talk about his book. Shouting above the black leather jacket crowd, I asked him about its publication on the Web. According to him, the Web was merely a convenient delivery vehicle, an easy way to distribute the book prior to its print publication to acquaintances asking for copies. But I am tempted to see in this publication history something more, a work that edged toward becoming a distributed multi-sited production, one of whose manifestations was a print book.

By this time I had taken to lurking on the *House of Leaves* website, where self-selected readers pursued the book with an intensity rivaling the most devoted literary critics, debating its intricacies with thousands of postings interrogating minute details. Evidently the book has become a cult phenomenon, attracting the same kind of devoted audience that *Gravity's Rainbow* won in the '70s and '80s. Judging from their rhetoric and interests, I guess that most of the website participants are young people between the ages of fifteen and thirty. I would die to have them as my students; they really care about this book. Their postings make clear that for them this literary text, rivaling in complexity works like Melville's *Moby Dick* or Joyce's *Ulysses*, is not a dusty classic but a vital living work they claim for their own.

My guesses were confirmed when Mark, fresh from a rock tour he took with his sister who sings under the name Poe, related the experience he had of running onto stage in the Dallas stadium to read the five-minute passage from *House of Leaves* that he and Poe recorded for their hit single "Hey Pretty." Eleven thousand fans, most under thirty, rose to their feet and gave him a standing ovation, roaring so loudly he was forced to wait several minutes before he could proceed. Complex literature as a rock performance? The phenomenon demands an explanation. I suspect the book has succeeded so wildly in part because it offers multiple paths into its complexities. It can be read on many levels, each offering specific pleasures. Straightforward action sequences appeal to fans neuronally challenged by too many Tom Cruise movies; the elaborate games and puzzles speak to the kind of users who spend months figuring out computer games like *Myst* and *Riven*; spoofs like the fake interviews with the glitterati, including Jacques Derrida, Andrew Ross and Camille Paglia, insinuate themselves with the cognoscenti; the complex narratives that emerge from Johnny Truant's footnotes and the letters of his mad mother, Pelafina, grab novel readers looking for psychologically complex characters and dense metaphoric patterns. For my part I like all of it, especially its encyclopedic impulse to make a world and encapsulate everything within its expanding perimeter, as if it were an exploding universe whose boundaries keep receding from the center with increasing velocity.

I was astonished to learn from Mark that the publisher accepted the manuscript when it was a continuous typescript, without any of the design elements that would become such a prominent feature of the published book. During production he tried to communicate to the press's designer what he had in mind and found it impossible; the design was too complex. So he flew to New York and sat for a month in the press's offices, typesetting the book himself on a computer. Upon first seeing the book, I thought it screamed "digital!", for it would have been almost impossible to set without a computer and certainly could not have sold for under twenty dollars. But in an interview with Larry McCafferey and Sinda Gregory that Larry generously shared with me prior to its publication, Mark makes a point of underplaying the role of the digital. He says "*HA!*" to critics who might think the book was written entirely on a computer, pointing out that he storyboarded the ferociously complex Chapter IX, where print runs riot in many directions on the page, entirely in pencil, a technology he praises for its robustness and reliability.

In that same interview, Danielewski relates a fascinating story about the book's origins that illuminates the privileged status it claims for print. His father was a mid-level filmmaker and a devoted student of the medium. He owned a projector and professional screen and would frequently bring films home for Mark and his sister to watch, even when they were very young. After dinner the father would put on a film and expect the children to view it with rapt attention. When it was over the father would grill them, asking detailed questions about edits, scene construction, and other technical matters (a practice that no doubt sheds light on the theme of narcissistic parents running through *House of Leaves*).

A crisis in the relationship came when Mark was in his early twenties and his father was hospitalized for prostate cancer, possibly terminal. Distraught, Mark channeled his intense emotions into a short story, "Redwood," a coded narrative about his relationship with his father. He showed it to his father in the hospital, who understood it was about their relationship. The father responded by becoming enraged, taunting Mark whether clear, reflective, insulated, heat-resistant, switchable, tinted, bad-guy, antique; or even tin-plated steel, factory-painted steel, brass; or even a single nail or screw, whether sheet-metal, particleboard, drywall, concrete, drive, aluminum, silicon bronze, solid brass, mechanically galvanized, yellow-zinc plated, stainless steel, epoxy coated, black finish, Durocoat; to say nothing of the sheer absence of anything that might suggest a roof, whether pitched, gable, hip, lean-to, flat, sawtooth, monitor, ogee, bell, dome, helm, sloped, hip-and-valley, conical, pavilion, rotunda,

famous expeditions where those involved con-
ces of depri-
elves caught

d Magellan
eda to sail
e and for all
tionize peo-
ut the jour-
with enough
would cost

five vessels
Bay of St.
ious. Fierce
to mention

ty of the future, had caused tensions among the
pril Fools Day, which also happened to be Easter
Concepcion and his servant Luiz de Molino
ng in the death of at least one officer and the
ately for Quesada, he never stopped to consider
lition to circle the globe could probably marshal
gross underestimation of his opponent cost Que-

se men still loyal to him to retake the comman-
l and his tactical acumen made his success, espe-
mutineer Mendoza of the *Victoria* was stabbed
rmed, and by morning the *Concepcion* had sur-
tiny had begun, Magellan was again in control.
and then in an act of calculated good-will sus-
concentrate maritime law and his own ire on the
g: Mendoza's corpse was drawn and quartered,

Juan de Cartagena was marooned on a barren shore and Quesada was executed.

Quesada, however, was not hung, shot or even forced to walk the plank. Magellan had a better idea. Molino, Quesada's trusty servant, was granted clemency if he agreed to execute his master. Molino accepted the duty and

Cabinet of Wonder, Jim Kalin's *One Worm*, Sartre's *Huis Clos*, or *Les Mouches*, Jules Verne's *Journey to the Center of the Earth*, Lem's *Solaris*, Ayn Rand's *The Fountainhead*, "The Turn of the Screw" by Henry James, Nathaniel Hawthorne's "Young Goodman Brown" or *The House of Seven Gables*, or *The Lion, the Witch and the Wardrobe* by C.S.

Of course, it is impossible to consider any sort of construction, whether of homes, factories, shops, stores, department stores, market halls, conservatories, exhibition buildings, railway stations, ware houses, and office buildings, exchanges, and banks, hotels, hospitals, museums, libraries, theatres, churches, bridges, airports, town halls, law courts, ministries and public offices, Houses of parliament, monuments, parks, even towns, and cities, public works etc., etc., without paying heed to such names as Thomas Hall Beeby, Ricardo Bofill, John Simpson, Steven Holl, Léon Krier, Richard Neutra, Andres Duany, and Elizabeth Plater-Zyberk, Ramon Fortet, Daniel Libeskind, Quinlan Terry, Allan Greenberg, Jane B. Drew, Robin Seifert, Frank Gehry, Jean Willerval, Arai Isozaki, Kisho Kurokawa, Gisue and Mojgan Hariri, John Outram, Zaha Hadid, Peter Eisenmann, Richard Meier, John Hejduk, Aldo Rossi, Herman Hertzberger, Louis E. Fry Sr., Louis E. Fry Jr., Louis E. Fry III, Santiago Calatrava, I. M. Pei, Ricardo Scofidio, Harry G. Robinson III, Terry Farrell, Bernard Tschumi, Charles F. McAfee, Eva Vecsei, the Coop by saying he should take quit wasting his time writing and get a job at the post office. Mark was so devastated he tore up the story and threw it in a dumpster. As far as he was concerned, that was the end of his writing career. A few days later his sister invited him to dinner. After a lovely meal, she presented him with a manila folder. He opened it to discover that she had retrieved the pieces of paper from the dumpster and painstakingly taped them back together. That rescued story became the kernel of *House of Leaves*.

The anecdote suggests that the book's remediation of film is, along with much else, the mark of a generational struggle, the son claiming the right to his own voice by encapsulating the father's medium within his. Moreover, although Danielewski has received several lucrative offers for movie options, he remains adamant that he will not allow the book to be made into a film. Unlike artists and writers who choose to work in digital media, Danielewski in his mid-thirties is young enough to take computers for granted. The daring move for him is not to adopt them but to return to the print book and re-invigorate it by extending its claims in relation to a plethora of competing media.

The remarkable achievement of *House of Leaves* is to devise a form that locates the book within the remediations of the digital era, along with the concomitant realization that reference becomes unstable or inaccessible in such an environment, and still deliver the pleasures of traditional realistic fiction. Evacuating the ORIGINARY SUBJECT, *House of Leaves* situates itself within the postmodern landscape but recovers an intensity of character and narrative through the processes of remediation themselves. The strategy is exemplified by the check mark that appears in the lower right corner of page 97. Before we arrive at this inscrutable sign, we read on page 72, in footnote 78, advice from "Ed." suggesting we skip forward to Appendix II E, the letters Pelafina writes to Johnny. If we follow this advice, we come upon the letter in which Pelafina, infected by growing paranoia, suspects the staff of interfering with her correspondence and asks Johnny to place a check mark in the lower right corner of his next letter if he has received her letter intact (p. 609). Breaking the boundary of the page, the check mark we see also crashes through the narratological structure that encapsulates Pelafina's letters within the higher ontological level of whomever arranges for the deceased woman's correspondence to be included in the manuscript (presumably Johnny) and the published book (presumably the editors).

The implications of these subversions are heightened by Pelafina's letter dated April 5, 1986, in which appears a semi-coherent series of phrases encapsulated within dashes. If we use the simple coding algorithm Pelafina suggests to Johnny in an earlier missive of forming messages by taking the first letter of each word, we are able to decode the sentence "My dear Zampano who did you lose?" (p. 615). The intimation that Pelafina can speak about Zampanò implies she may be the writer who creates both the old man's narrative and her son's commentary. Combined with the check mark, this coded message suggests that apparently distinct ontological levels can melt into one another. The subversion includes the reality that we as readers inhabit, for the page margins into which the check mark intrudes exist in a space contiguous with our world and *House of Leaves* as a book we can hold in our hands.

These paradoxical inversions prepare us for the unforgettable scene in which Navidson, deep in the bowels of the House and floating suspended in space, uses precious matches (which have their own history) to read the book *House of Leaves*. When he is down to his last match he lights the page, his eyes desperately racing to finish before the fire consumes it (pp. 465–67). The image of him reading the story that contains him presents us with a vivid warning that this book threatens always to break out of the cover that binds it. It is an artifact fashioned to consume the reader even as the reader consumes it. We cannot say we have not been warned. We have seen the writing devour Zampanò's life, render Johnny an obsessional wreck, and compel Navidson to reenter the House though he knows he may die in the attempt. This is a technotext so energetic, labyrinthine, and impossible to command that we will not be able to leave it alone because it will not leave us alone. It grabs us, sucks out our center, and gives us back to ourselves through multiple remediations, transforming us in the process.

In these posthuman days, *House of Leaves* demonstrates that technologies do not simply inscribe preexisting thoughts. Rather, artifacts such as this book serve as noisy channels of communication in which messages are transformed and enfolded together as they are encoded and decoded, mediated and remediated. *House of Leaves* implicitly refutes the position Claude Shannon assigns to humans in his famous communication diagram, in which they are positioned outside the channel and labeled "sender" and "receiver." As readers enmeshed in the book, we find ourselves positioned, like Will Navidson, *inside* the book we read, receiving messages to be sure but also constituted by the messages that percolate through the intersecting circulatory pathways of the book called *House of Leaves*.

The implication for studies of technology and literature is that the materiality of inscription thoroughly interpenetrates the represented world. Even when technology does not appear as a theme, it is woven into the fictional world through the *processes* that produce the literary work as a material artifact. *House of Leaves* provides a powerful example showing why a fully adequate theory of semiotics must take into account the materiality of inscription technologies as well as a material understanding of the signifier. Technological effects can no more be separated from literary effects than characters can be separated from the writings that contain and are contained by them. Through its material metaphors, *House of Leaves* suggests that the appropriate model for subjectivity is a communication circuit rather than discrete individualism, for narration remediation rather than representation, and for reading and writing inscription technology fused with consciousness rather than a mind conveying its thoughts directly to the reader.

Focusing on materiality allows us to see the dynamic interactivity through which a literary work mobilizes its physical embodiment in conjunction with its verbal signifiers to construct meanings in ways that implicitly construct the user/reader as well. It is no accident that electronic texts such as *Lexia to Perplexia*, artists' books like *A Humument*, and print novels like *House of Leaves* envision subjects who are formed through and with the inscription technologies these works employ. The writing machines that physically create fictional subjects through inscriptions also connect us as readers to the interfaces, print and electronic, that transform us by reconfiguring our interactions with their materialities. Inscribing consequential fictions, writing machines reach through the inscriptions they write and that write them to re-define what it means to write, to read, and to be human.

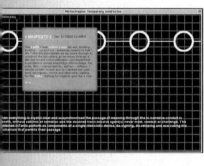

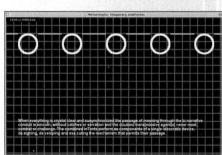

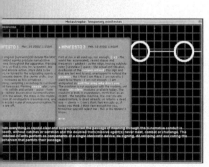

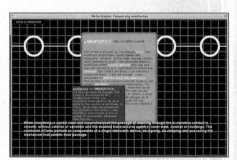

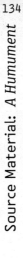

Source Material: *A Humument*

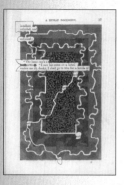

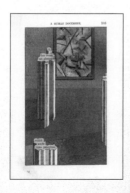

Source Material: House of Leaves

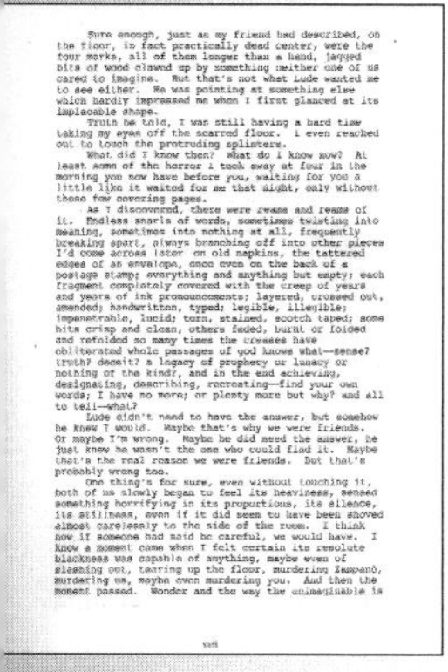

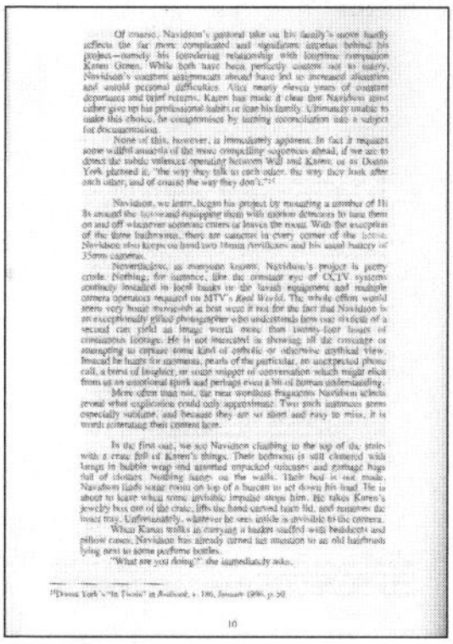

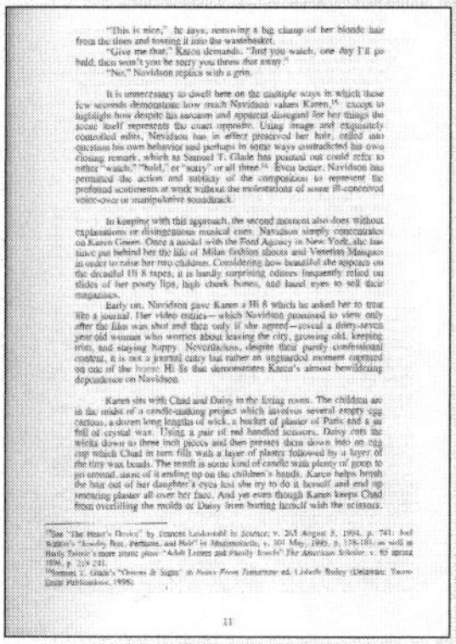

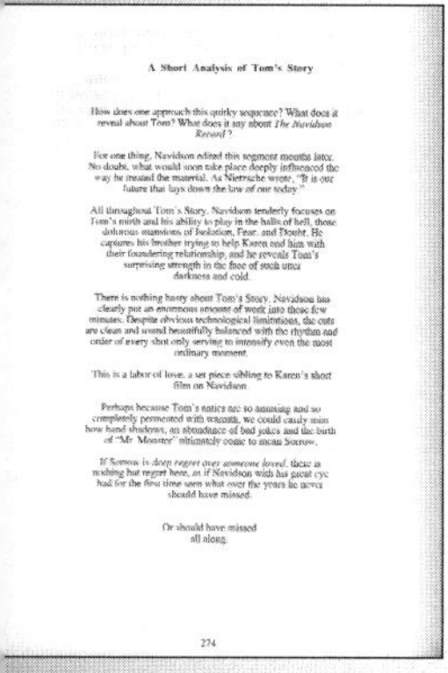

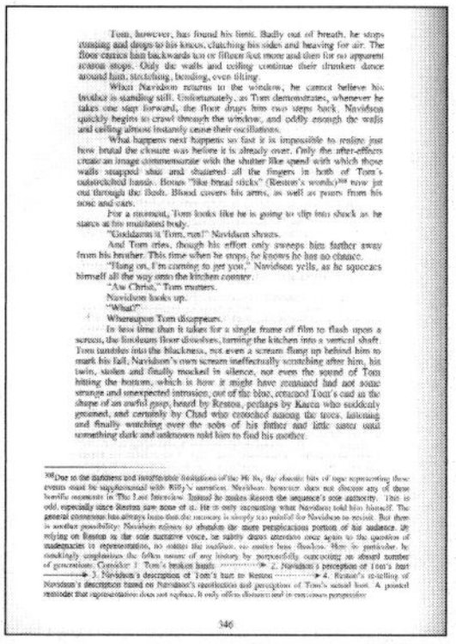

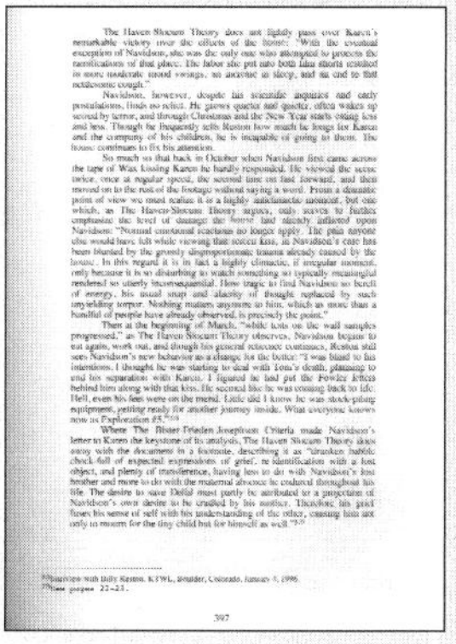

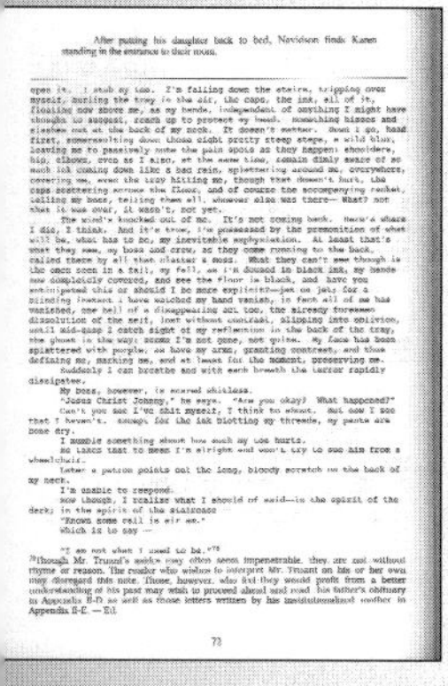

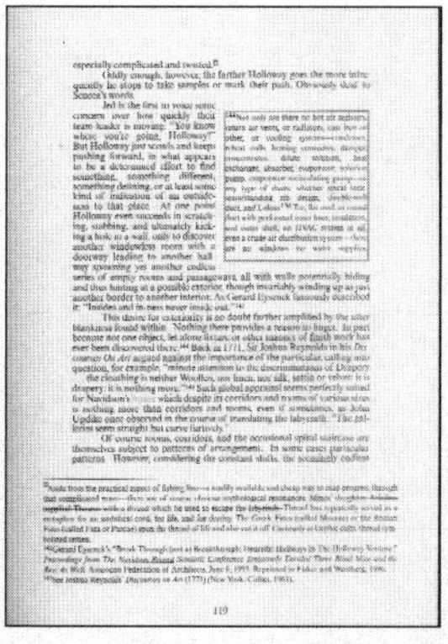

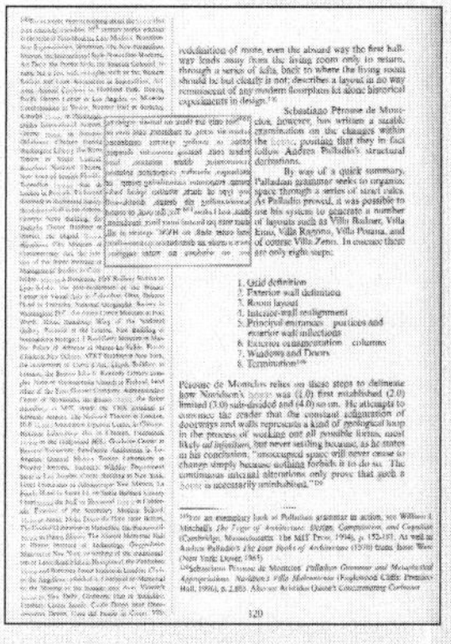

Endtroduction

With *Writing Machines,* the Mediawork Pamphlet series becomes even more explicit in its goal of producing theoretical fetish objects with visual, tactile, and yes, intellectual appeal. Because, what is a fetish, after all, but an object imbued with fantasy, a thing that links outside itself to powerful imaginary realms? It's no wonder that one of the chief fetishes our society has produced is the book. But bibliomaniacal impulses are mutating in this world of multi–, trans–, inter–, and re–mediation, and we need to establish new categories for describing the emotional and physical relationships readers have with what (and how) they read.

The emergence of computer mediated communication has affected not just our ideas about the world, but also the forms they take. In *Writing Machines,* N. Katherine Hayles has woven together the modes of intellectualized theory and personalized narrative, the cultures of science and the humanities, and through her collaboration with Anne Burdick, the mandates of writing and design. I can imagine no team better suited for such a project.

Professor of English and Design | Media Arts at the University of California at Los Angeles, N. Katherine Hayles (Kate to her friends) is our most significant thinker about the intersection of literature and technology, from *The Cosmic Web: Scientific Field Models and Literary Strategies in the Twentieth Century* (1984), through her groundbreaking work *Chaos Bound: Orderly Disorder in Contemporary Literature and Science* (1990) and the edited collection *Chaos and Disorder: Complex Dynamics in Literature and Science* (1990), to *How We Became Posthuman: Virtual Bodies in Cybernetics, Literature, and Informatics* (1999) which won both the Rene Wellek Prize for the best book in literary theory and the Eaton Award for the best book on science fiction theory and criticism. With the polemical little book you have in your hands, Kate makes the case that thinking about literature without thinking about materiality isn't really thinking at all.

Anne Burdick's triple threat practice—she designs, writes, and/or edits client-based and self-initiated projects out of the Offices of Anne Burdick—

made her the ideal choice for *Writing Machines*. The plurality of "Offices" goes beyond the binary of practice and theory, enfolding what might be termed Anne's entrepreneurial approach to broadening the parameters of contemporary design. Anne is the site designer and design editor of the online literary journal, *electronicbookreview.com*. She designed the *Fackel Wörterbuch: Redensarten* (2000), an unconventional 1,056-page dictionary created in collaboration with literary scientists at the Austrian Academy of Sciences, which won "The Most Beautiful Book in the World" prize at the 2001 Leipzig book fair. Currently, Anne is a core faculty member in the graduate Media Design Program at Art Center College of Design, and also teaches at the California Institute of the Arts.

Together, Kate and Anne have created both a book and an object, ideas embedded in visual language, narratives embodied between covers, flowing over printed surfaces. They mount a brilliant defense against the instant nostalgia which posits a golden age just passed—a golden age of literature, or of electronic literature, or of a perfectly unmediated existence.

Major ongoing funding for the Mediawork Pamphlet series comes from the Rockefeller Foundation. The first three Pamphlets are supported by a start-up grant from Jeffrey and Catharine Soros. Additional funding has been provided by the Office of the President, Art Center College of Design. Doug Sery at The MIT Press continues to offer support and inspiration. I'd like to thank Andy Davidson for his friendship and support over the years. And for their help launching this series, I'd like to acknowledge Brenda Laurel and Denise Gonzales Crisp, author and designer respectively of the first Mediawork pamplet, *Utopian Entrepreneur* (2001). I'm appreciative of the work that Triplecode's David Young and Pascal Wever put into the Mediawork Web site, and to Scott McCloud for setting the bar so high with the first WebTake, "Idea Tree." You can see all of their work and more at MITPRESS.MIT.EDU/MEDIAWORK, including the WebTake for *Writing Machines*.

Peter Lunenfeld, Editorial Director

Designer's Notes

New types of criticism require new forms, which require new ways of working. In order to create a book that embodies its own critical concepts—a technotext—it is imperative that the design evolves in tandem with the text. The Mediawork series fosters such cooperation, which allowed me to work as a designer *with* words rather than *after* words, the usual chain of command. Thanks to Kate Hayles's intellectual generosity and Peter Lunenfeld's vision for the series, the design of *Writing Machines* was able to become more than a visual translation alone: it's a critical investigation, a Media-Specific Analysis in more ways than one.

Kate's critical framework challenged me to create a book that re–presents itself, over and over: as a tool for storage and retrieval, as the first home of Literature, as a navigational device, a writing space, and a representation of knowledge. The material metaphors that result work and rework the body of the codex, amplifying the book's status *as a book*.

The referential imagery that accumulates on the surface of each page includes visual <u>SAMPLES</u> from the three central projects under consideration—*Lexia to Perplexia*, *A Humument*, and *House of Leaves*—a design–writing strategy that exposes the shortcomings of certain word-centric scholarly conventions. Folding the pages of these projects into the pages of *Writing Machines* created its own set of difficulties, but in the process it revealed much about the complex relationship between showing and telling, from the role of context in quotations to the ways in which we read.

The table of contents, the <u>LEXICON LINKMAP</u> and its counterpart at <u>MITPRESS.MIT.EDU/MEDIAWORK</u>, the samples and the <u>SOURCE MATERIAL</u> that gives them context, and the <u>AFFORDANCES</u> (those amplified entry points into the text) each offer an alternate view of the conceptual terrain of the book. (And they reflect my own interest in <u>SPATIAL WRITING</u> and <u>WORD MAPS</u>—new names for underused forms that have found in Hayles's text a type of criticism that fits.) These refractions make visible different aspects of the writing's internal rhythms, organizational logic, and theoretical orientation.

When searching for the right typefaces to identify the two voices that Kate braids into a third, I longed for a working version of Typalette and Font Sculptor, a prototype software project developed by Cynthia Jacquette. Typalette is a type catalog and search tool that allows the user to find fonts based on "look" (contrast, weight, serifs, etc.), "facts" (historical context, type designer, etc.), and—significantly—"feel" (rural, aggressive, precious, and so forth). If a typeface doesn't exist that matches your selected attributes, Font Sculptor will make a custom face that does.

Fortunately Cynthia works with me now, and she could perform the tasks that her prototype could only promise. She located the typeface Cree Sans for the personal and Egyptienne for the theoretical. Then she melded the two to create Creegyptienne, the synthesized voice of the personal–theoretical, the "soft serif" font that you are reading now. While the subtle typographic coding may not be recognized by every reader, we felt that a synthesis more accurately reflected the writing than did the fragmentation of a hybrid.

Working with such a provocative critic as Kate, one whose opinions are strong and generous in equal measure, was a pleasure, a learning experience, and an honor. A successful design–writing collaboration requires an editor who addresses each realm with equal interest. Peter Lunenfeld is an exception in the scholarly world: he is a true advocate of the cultural contributions that design can make. His voice and support are invaluable—as evidenced by this pamphlet series. I am grateful to Peter for inviting me to be a part of this important project, and especially for pairing me with Kate.

On the personal level, I have to say that smack in the middle of designing this book I bought a house, gave birth to a son, and built and moved into a new studio. I couldn't have done it all *and* completed this project *and* kept my sanity without the understanding of Peter and Kate, Cynthia's talent and good humor, or the love and support of my mother, Marcia Ackleson, and my partner, Roy Morris.

Anne Burdick

Author's Acknowledgements

This book was born when Peter Lunenfeld made the trek over to the West Side of Los Angeles to talk about his idea for small-format books, with extensive visual content, scheduled to appear in a new series at MIT Press. I listened with excitement, seeing in his offer an opportunity to explore the interaction of words with images that had already attracted my attention in electronic media. When he told me that I would be limited to 110 pages of manuscript, I thought, "This will be easy—something I could whip off in three or four months." What I mistook for the buzzing bloom of a spring day was, I would discover three or four months later, the laughter of the gods at another mortal madly deceived. As fall deepened into winter, I continued apace with the theoretical and critical readings of the literature, but the autobiographical component Peter insisted the book should have eluded me. I toyed with various schemes, inserting personal passages, alluding to past events, but none satisfied me. They seemed tacked-on, beside the point, feeble in comparison to the clarity and precision of theoretical analysis.

As the new year dawned I was close to despair. I considered telling Peter that I could not do autobiography, that he should ditch this project and go on to someone more skilled in the art of self-revelation. Then I heard J. Hillis Miller deliver a wonderful paper in which he invented autobiographical personae, based on him and his grandson, to explore the differences between a generation raised with print versus one raised with computers. Suddenly I knew how to solve my problem; I could invent a persona. The solution was laughably obvious, the first lesson of Fiction 101, but it had taken me months to work through the barriers I had thrown up around the idea of autobiography so I could finally see it. With that realization, the words came tumbling out in a flow I felt I was not so much inventing as barely controlling in its exuberant engagement.

My next challenge was the length restriction that at first had made the project seem easy. I had written at least twice that amount, and now the problem was condensing without losing the density that appealed to me. Peter played a major role, intervening in ways that reminded me of editors in times gone by, when the editor did not merely rubber-stamp a completed manuscript but actively worked with the author to create the final product. For his good sense and editorial intuition, I am profoundly in his debt. Also important were Anne Burdick's insights. More than any of us, Anne remained alert to the material qualities of the texts I was discussing and producing, pointing out places where descriptions needed to be more concrete, engaging, and specific in their attention to materiality.

I still have lingering regret that the series format does not allow footnotes and other scholarly apparatus. As a compromise, we are posting them on the web site associated with the book. I encourage readers to consult MITPRESS.MIT.EDU/MEDIAWORK, where I acknowledge the extensive debts I owe to scholars, critics, theorists and writers. To Marjorie Luesebrink, who read drafts and offered warm support, I am deeply grateful for her insights and friendship. I benefited from conversations with Doug Sery, Robert Coover, Michael Joyce, David Platzker, Joan Lyons, Tom Mitchell, Mark Danielewski, Jay Bolter, Richard Grusin, Rita Raley, Bill Seaman and John Johnston. Espen Aarseth, Jerome McGann, Johanna Drucker, and Matthew Kirschenbaum inspired me with their pioneering work in materialist criticism. M. D. Coverley, Talan Memmott, Diana Slattery, Adriana de Souza e Silva and Fabian Winkler graciously gave permission to quote from emails and essays and use images from their works. Michael Fadden and Carol Wald contributed essential research assistance. I am grateful to the Museum of Modern Art in New York City and Getty Research Library for access to their collections. Portions of Chapter 6 first appeared in *Narrative*, Chapter 4 in the SIGGRAPH *Electronic Catalogue* and *Digital Creativity*, and Chapter 8 in *American Literature*, and I am grateful to them for permission to reprint. I deeply appreciate a fellowship from the National Endowment for the Humanities and the University of California, Los Angeles Senate Research Grant. My greatest debt is to Nicholas Gessler for innumerable discussions and the use of his DSL connection.

N. Katherine Hayles

The MIT Press
Cambridge, Massachusetts
London, England

Writing Machines
by N. Katherine Hayles

a MEDIAWORK pamphlet
MITPRESS.MIT.EDU/MEDIAWORK

Printed and bound
in the United States of America.

Library of Congress Control Number:
2002113867
ISBN 0-262-58215-5